HOW
CAN I UNDERSTAND
THE
BIBLE
?

BILL BRIGHT

HARVEST HOUSE PUBLISHERS
EUGENE, OREGON

D0526665

Unless otherwise indicated, all Scripture quotations are from the Holy Bible, New Living Translation, copyright © 1996, 2004, 2007, 2013 by Tyndale House Foundation. Used by permission of Tyndale House Publishers, Inc., Carol Stream, Illinois 60188. All rights reserved.

Verses marked NIV are from the Holy Bible, New International Version®, NIV®. Copyright © 1973, 1978, 1984, 2011 by Biblica, Inc.® Used by permission. All rights reserved worldwide.

Verses marked NASB are from the New American Standard Bible ®, © 1960, 1962, 1963, 1968, 1971, 1972, 1973, 1975, 1977, 1995 by The Lockman Foundation. Used by permission. (www.Lockman.org)

Verses marked NKJV are from the New King James Version®. Copyright © 1982 by Thomas Nelson, Inc. Used by permission. All rights reserved.

Cover by Knail

HOW CAN I UNDERSTAND THE BIBLE?
Copyright © 2004 Bright Media Foundation
Published by Harvest House Publishers
Eugene, Oregon 97402
www.harvesthousepublishers.com

Library of Congress Cataloging-in-Publication Data
    Bright, Bill.
    [Discover the book God wrote]
    How can I understand the Bible? / Bill Bright.
        pages cm
    Originally published under title: Discover the book God wrote. Wheaton, Ill. : Tyndale House Publishers, c2004.
    Includes bibliographical references.
    ISBN 978-0-7369-6619-1 (pbk.)
    ISBN 978-0-7369-6620-7 (eBook)
    1. Bible—Introductions. I. Title.
    BS475.3.B75 2016
    220.6'1—dc23
                                                    2015025422

All rights reserved. No part of this publication may be reproduced, stored in a retrieval system, or transmitted in any form or by any means—electronic, mechanical, digital, photocopy, recording, or any other—except for brief quotations in printed reviews, without the prior permission of the publisher.

Printed in the United States of America
        16 17 18 19 20 21 22 23 24 / BP-JC / 10 9 8 7 6 5 4 3 2 1

Contents

Acknowledgments

Bill Bright's personal walk with Jesus Christ made an indelible imprint on my life. For more than three decades I observed the life of a man who believed every word of the Bible and lived a life of faith that often stretched the faith of those who walked with him.

The last weeks of Bill's life were filled with phone calls and bedside meetings, giving directions and challenges to those of us who would attempt to carry out his plans. I will remember always the many times a nurse would call me in to meet with Bill, and upon entering the room, I would find him smiling, holding his Bible, and on some occasions, asleep with his open Bible on his chest.

On Dr. Bright's behalf, I dedicate this book to every person who will read it and catch a glimpse of the passion Bill had for the Word of God. The Bright Media Foundation was established with the purpose of continuing the ministry of Dr. Bright and sharing his passion for Christ. Vonette Bright is living proof of the sustaining power in the Word of God. She shared with Bill the commitment to the truth of God's Word for over fifty years and now moves forward with renewed faith.

Helmut Teichert's oversight of projects for the Bright Media Foundation gave Bill great confidence. Dr. Bright was a great encourager, and he often expressed his heartfelt thanks to Brenda Josee for her commitment to the accurate representation of his beliefs. John Barber spent many hours in the initial development of the manuscript.

Joette Whims and Lynn Vanderzalm provided valuable editorial work on this project.

I cannot conclude my expressions without thanking Vonette Bright for her demonstration of a life of faith that gives all of us confidence and excitement to press on with great passion to extend the legacy of Dr. Bill Bright.

John Nill, CEO
Bright Media Foundation

INTRODUCTION

Discover the Treasure
of Your Life

Have you ever dreamed of discovering something that would be worth a fortune? All of us have heard stories about someone who found a treasure in an attic or in a box forgotten in an aunt's basement. One television show, *Antiques Roadshow,* travels around the country stopping at many places and allowing people to bring in their antiques for appraisal by experts. Once in a while, the show unearths a valuable artifact, thrilling the owners.

Some time ago, a true-life story of a magnificent find hit the national news. It started in the mid-1990s when a female trucker named Teri was traveling through the Southwest and stopped to meander through Dot's Thrift Shop near San Bernardino, California. She spotted a colorful painting and thought it would make a great gag gift for a friend who was having difficulties. Teri bought the painting for five dollars.

What a buy it turned out to be. Ten years later, art experts concluded that the painting was created in the 1940s by Jackson Pollock, a leading American artist. His "drip paintings" are so unique that they are almost impossible to imitate or forge. Art restoration expert Peter Paul Biro examined the painting and found a partial fingerprint that he compared to a known fingerprint of Pollock and noted twelve characteristics that are identical between the two prints. Biro also writes that the paint and the style used are just like Pollock's.

Although no one can be sure how the painting got to the thrift store, it most likely was purchased in an estate sale in Victorville, California.

Wrapped in burlap and covered with dust and spider webs, it was a gem shrouded in secrecy, a gem that even the owner of Dot's Thrift Store failed to recognize. Yet one estimate is that the painting may be worth as much as twenty-five million dollars.

Can you imagine what Teri felt when she first had an inkling of the painting's value? I can imagine her calling her friends and exclaiming, "Guess what—that old painting I got at the thrift store turns out to be a treasure!" What had seemed at first to be just a run-of-the-mill purchase was truly a fine work of art.

A Treasure in Disguise

That story reminds me of a discovery I made years ago.[1] As a high school and college student I occasionally tried to read the Bible, but it made no sense to me. I found it boring and concluded that no intelligent person could ever believe what it said. I certainly didn't think that the Bible was trustworthy.

Then I became a Christian. From that moment, my life was transformed, and my attitude concerning the Scriptures changed dramatically. It was as if the Holy Spirit had unwrapped God's words from a covering of dusty burlap, and I discovered what a treasure I had in my hands. I realized that the Bible was truly the holy, inspired, and infallible Word of the greatest author in the universe, our Father God.

Since that great discovery, I have spent nearly sixty years studying the Bible, including five years of theological study at Princeton and Fuller Theological Seminaries. One of the important things I learned in seminary was a greater and more profound respect for the Bible. Even more significant, I have seen in my own life—and in the lives of so many others—what the Bible can do. Today my excitement over the Bible is undiminished. Indeed, it grows with each passing day.

I praise God that He used His Word to change me dramatically. As a young man, I was especially ambitious. I was a humanist and a materialist. The only way I knew of measuring success was through the accumulation of wealth. And that's what I was doing. I started my own fancy foods business and put all my energies into making it a financial success. But with the prompting of the Holy Spirit and through my study of God's Word, I began to learn about our great God and Savior, why He came in the person of Jesus of Nazareth to this planet Earth, and all that He accomplished for me. Over time as I studied and read, the great benefits of receiving Jesus as my Savior and Lord and walking with Him daily began to become more and more real to me. I learned that all the blessings of heaven could be added to me if I would faithfully seek first the kingdom of God and His righteousness. This revolutionized my life. In time, the desire to get rich waned, and the thrill of serving God and seeing eternal results superseded my other ambitions.

Today I cannot imagine returning to my self-centered plans. Over the years I've come to the conclusion that I would be the fool of fools to do anything that would rob me of the incredible privilege of living in the light of God's Word and enjoying the supernatural adventure of walking in fellowship with Him. Each day is an opportunity to be part of His great strategy to share His love with all people everywhere in fulfillment of the Great Commission. Discovering God through the Bible has been the greatest find of my life.

Since 1945, I have known many of the world's rich, famous, and powerful people. Many of them achieved what I dreamed of doing as a young man—and are as unhappy as ever without God. I can assure you from experience and observation, true happiness comes from loving God with all of our hearts, souls, minds, and strength, and seeking first His kingdom. I know without a doubt that I made the right choice.

Even today I live every moment with the Bible. It is my constant companion. As a believer for fifty-six years, I have tested God's Word and found it true. In more than five decades I have not encountered one situation in which I have not been able to turn to God's Word for comfort, wisdom, guidance, joy, and blessing.

At eighty-one years of age, I would rather have the Bible on my shelf and in my heart than any other book written in history because it contains the message of God to me and to all other human beings, who are created in His image. Not only have I been transformed and enriched through reading the Bible, but I have also seen it change the lives of multitudes of people.

The Book of Your Life

At this point you may be thinking, *It's easy for you to understand the Bible. You had seminary training and have studied the Scriptures for years. But I don't have those advantages. I want to know what God says to me, but reading the Bible seems so difficult. I have trouble finding a Bible reference when my pastor reads from the Bible, especially if the passage comes from the Old Testament. When I read the Bible myself, I can't understand how the ideas apply to me.*

I understand your situation. I had the same perspective when I first discovered the Bible. And I want you to overcome those difficulties. That's why I wrote this book. I want to share with you easy ways to make the Bible the book of your life. Rather than merely telling you about the content of the Bible, I want this book to give you a start in reading and studying the Bible on your own. With this ability, you will see the Lord transform your life through His Word and His Spirit. God works uniquely in each of our lives, and He will emphasize different parts of His message for you because He knows and sees your unique personality, situations, and needs. If you can learn how to mine God's Word for yourself and find the countless treasures He has for you, you will have a lifetime of adventure in walking with God.

Keep in mind that God's great desire is to reveal Himself to us. One of the most heartwarming and inspiring life stories of the twentieth century is that of the remarkable Helen Keller. If you remember, she was blind and deaf, and everyone assumed she would live out her life in darkness and ignorance. Then her parents hired a teacher, Anne Sullivan, who pierced the shroud that enveloped the child by introducing her to words and thereby to communication. Using a unique form of "finger language," Anne began spelling words into the child's hand, and eventually Helen recognized the link between the words and objects. Once Anne Sullivan had given Helen the names of several physical objects, Miss Sullivan attempted to explain the existence of God. She tapped out the symbols for the name *God.*

Much to Miss Sullivan's surprise, Helen spelled back, "Thank you for telling me God's name, Teacher, for He has touched me many times before." Even in her darkness, Helen Keller already knew that God existed. With the help of Anne Sullivan, the young blind girl had the ability to "see" and learn more about who God is and what He does for us.

Each of us has an inborn spiritual need to know God, but we must go beyond our soul's instinct to find out the specific details of what He is like and what He has done. The primary way we discover God's nature is through the Bible. It is His special revelation to us, His way of communicating with us.

One thing I have learned over the years is that the Bible is a living book. The apostle John writes these intriguing lines: "In the beginning was the Word, and the Word was with God, and the Word was God. He was with God in the beginning" (John 1:1-2 NIV). This is a mysterious and supernatural concept. The *Word* in this verse refers to Jesus Christ. John is saying that the text of the Bible is not just black ink on white paper, but it is infused with the character and message of Jesus Christ, who is the visible image of God. When we read the Bible, we discover the very essence of God's nature.

Does this excite you as it does me? No other book can make this claim. The Bible is so interconnected with God that we cannot separate it from His being. When we read the Bible with the right attitude, God, in the person of the Holy Spirit, joins with our spirit to help us understand it and apply it. The book comes alive. The words in the Bible have life-changing power.

What Is the Bible?

Let me start our treasure hunt by giving you some facts that show the Bible's influence. It is by far the best-selling book of all time. No other book comes close in the number of copies printed, distributed, reprinted, and passed down from one generation to the next. This remarkable book has been translated into more than fourteen hundred languages and dialects. People of extremely diverse backgrounds wrote it over a period of fifteen hundred years, and yet all sixty-six books of the Bible are uniquely in accord with each other. And there are more books written about the Bible than about any other work in the history of mankind. God's holy and inspired Word towers above every other volume in its positive impact on individuals and nations.

The Bible is the cornerstone of Western civilization. Let me give you one of my favorite examples. George Washington, one of the greatest figures in American history, was a man completely devoted to God and to His Word. Washington said, "It is impossible to rightly govern the world without God and the Bible."[2] The first American president lived this out. From his youth, George Washington began and ended every day on his knees, reading his Bible and praying for God's guidance and blessing. He taught the American troops that God's Word was the standard to live by. What a tremendous example.

Mining for Treasure

When approaching the Bible, we must recognize that it has a definite form and organization. Understanding this format will help us in our reading and study. To give you an overview of what is in the Bible, I have included four sections in this book.

Part 1—"Why Should I Believe the Bible?"—gives important information about the Bible's author and the Scriptures' reliability, basic message, and promises. Each chapter concludes with a section called Discover the Treasure, which includes material to help you dig into God's Word for yourself. The discovery material in the next chapter will give a map of the major sections of the Bible. The next two chapters will help you establish a habit of reading and memorizing Scripture and of using Scripture to build a more effective prayer life.

Part 2—"How Can I Understand the Bible?"—gives the basic elements of how to study the Bible and apply what you learn. The discovery material includes simple Bible studies for you to try on your own.

Part 3—"What Is the Bible About?"—presents an amazing look at who God is and how we can respond to Him. The discovery material includes simple Bible studies that will illuminate God's roles as Creator, Judge, and Savior.

By the time you reach Part 4—"How Does the Bible Change My Life?"—you will begin to feel more comfortable about using your Bible. You will be ready for these practical chapters on how the Bible builds faith, power, holiness, and love in our hearts and relationships. The discovery material that accompanies these chapters leads you through several biographical studies.

The discovery material at the end of this introductory chapter will help you select a Bible if you don't already have a favorite version. You will also get a glimpse of the differences between several versions of the Bible. I encourage you to select one main version to use in your study but also have on hand several others so that you can compare passages of Scripture from time to time. Most of the verses quoted in this book are from the New Living Translation of the Bible. All others are marked.

Beginning the Adventure

At this point, you may be thinking, *This sounds so hard. I'm not sure I can do it all.* Take heart. The steps to the Bible studies in this book are simple, clear, and short. They are written with not only the beginner in mind but also the person who has a busy schedule and still wants to make reading and studying Scripture a priority.

This is not a deep theological book that digs out the most difficult concepts in the Bible. What I want above all is to give you the basic tools to help you begin your adventure with the Bible. God is so practical, and He wants us to live a glorious life. There is so much we can learn about who we are in God's eyes and what He wants to do through us. Your life can truly be transformed by God's Word, as mine has been.

Since I became a follower of Jesus, the desire of my heart has been to please Him, to love Him, to trust Him, and to obey Him. Christ, in turn, has graciously caused my faith to grow and my relationship with Him to be enhanced. Now I find that having walked with Jesus for nearly sixty years, I am far more in love with Him, more excited about Him, and more enthusiastic about sharing my faith in Christ with others with every passing day. So you can see why I am so excited about the Scriptures. This is where I learn of His love for me and how I can love and serve Him and others better.

My goal through this book is to encourage a true "revival of the Bible" in your life. Certainly the Bible contains far more than what I have condensed in these pages. Let this book inspire you to learn all you can about God's supernatural Word so that you can go on to spend a wonderful lifetime of discovering God's treasures. You will be the richer for it.

Before you turn to the next page, stop and ask God to open your heart and mind to understanding the marvelous gift of Scripture. In our sinful condition, we cannot change ourselves. But through opening ourselves to the work of God's Spirit and reliance on God's Word, He will do the changing in us.

The Bible is the greatest treasure you will ever own. It is priceless. What a tragedy it would be if you let its cover accumulate dust on a bookshelf through neglect. I encourage you to treasure the Bible as the greatest source of hope, strength, encouragement, peace, and blessing known to mankind.

DISCOVER THE TREASURE

Spending time with your own Bible is an important way of learning about God through His Word. The Bible is the most important book you will own, and it's important that you have the right one for your needs. If you don't own a Bible that helps you want to read God's Word, consider the options we discuss in the following paragraphs.

Since the Bible was written mostly in Hebrew and Greek, our English versions are translations that biblical scholars have made from the original languages, preferably from the most reliable manuscripts available. The scholars who work on a translation of the Bible must follow certain defined translation rules to ensure the accuracy of the English text.

Translators use one of two methods in translating the Scriptures: *formal equivalence* or *dynamic (functional) equivalence*. Formal equivalence tries to render a word-for-word equivalent of the original language. Dynamic equivalence tries to render a thought-for-thought equivalence of the original language, an attempt to recreate the same dynamic impact on modern readers as the original text had on its readers.[3]

I recommend reading the Bible in several translations, chosen for the unique characteristics of each Bible. By using different translations, you will gain a fuller understanding of the meaning of the original text. The list below will help you with selecting the right Bibles, and the comparisons of translations will give you a flavor of the differences you will encounter.

When you are doing devotional reading, you may at times want to use a paraphrase, which is sometimes easier to understand. I have enjoyed using the Living Bible as a paraphrase that speaks to my heart.

When choosing a Bible, also consider using a study Bible. Study Bibles come in various translations and include not only the full biblical text but also study notes, maps, time lines, outlines, and other helpful tools.

Technology has had a great impact on the resources available to study the Bible. A typical Bible-study software package offers thousands of commentary notes from dozens of Bible reference works for a fraction of the price of owning all of the separate resources. With many Bible software programs, you can instantly search everyday topics—such as love, friendship, or troubles—to find out what the Bible says about such topics. Plus, with a visually animated Bible, you can explore virtual re-creations of the world of the Bible—the streets of Jerusalem, the Temple, and the Tabernacle. Such visual and written resources are invaluable for understanding the context of Bible passages and their meaning. A solid Bible software package is a great start for a home Bible reference library and a powerful tool for understanding God's Word.

The following list describes the main versions of the English Bible used today.[4] Consider them when you purchase a new Bible. Then make that Bible your own. Underline key passages that speak to you. Make notes in the margins. Record dates of the times you claim a promise found in a certain verse. Read and hear the words in your Bible as a love letter from your heavenly Father.

Strictly literal
English Standard Version (ESV)
New American Standard Bible (NASB)

Literal
> King James Version (KJV)
> New King James Version (NKJV)
> Revised Standard Version (RSV)

Literal with freedom to be idiomatic
> New Revised Standard Version (NRSV)

Thought-for-thought
> New International Version (NIV)
> New Jerusalem Bible (NJB)
> Revised English Bible (REB)

Dynamic (functionally) equivalent (modern speech)
> Today's English Version (TEV)
> New Living Translation (NLT)
> Contemporary English Version (CEV)

Paraphrastic
> The Living Bible (TLB)
> The Message (MSG)

Looking at how various Bibles render the same passage can give you a sense of the distinctives of the various translations. Read how several Bibles (in alphabetical order) render this passage from John 1:1-5:

English Standard Version

> In the beginning was the Word, and the Word was with God, and the Word was God. He was in the beginning with God. All things were made through him, and without him was not any thing made that was made. In him was life, and the life was the light of men. The light shines in the darkness, and the darkness has not overcome it.

King James Version

In the beginning was the Word, and the Word was with God, and the Word was God.

The same was in the beginning with God.

All things were made by him; and without him was not any thing made that was made.

In him was life; and the life was the light of men.

And the light shineth in darkness; and the darkness comprehended it not.

The Living Bible

Before anything else existed, there was Christ, with God. He has always been alive and is himself God. He created everything there is—nothing exists that he didn't make. Eternal life is in him, and this life gives light to all mankind. His life is the light that shines through the darkness—and the darkness can never extinguish it.

New International Version

In the beginning was the Word, and the Word was with God, and the Word was God. He was with God in the beginning. Through him all things were made; without him nothing was made that has been made. In him was life, and that life was the light of all mankind. The light shines in the darkness, but the darkness has not overcome it.

New Living Translation

In the beginning the Word already existed.
   The Word was with God,
   and the Word was God.
He existed in the beginning with God.
God created everything through him,
   and nothing was created except through him.

The Word gave life to everything that was created,
    and his life brought light to everyone.
The light shines in the darkness,
    and the darkness can never extinguish it.

New Revised Standard Version

In the beginning was the Word, and the Word was with God, and the Word was God. He was in the beginning with God. All things came into being through him, and without him not one thing came into being. What has come into being in him was life, and the life was the light of all people. The light shines in the darkness, and the darkness did not overcome it.

PART 1

Why Should I Believe the Bible?

*"Holy Scripture is the preeminent authority
for every Christian, and the rule of faith
and of all human perfection."*

JOHN WYCLIFFE

1

Who Wrote the Bible?

How essential is the Bible to you? What would you give up to keep it? Your reputation? Your friends? How about your freedom?

The English Bible did not come to us without a price. John Wycliffe sacrificed all the things above so that the people of England could read the Bible in their own language. His story is inspiring.

Wycliffe lived in the 1300s, when most people in Europe were poor and uneducated. Life was so hard that everyday living consumed all their energy. They had little time left for leisure or schooling. Even if they could get their hands on a Bible, it was written in Latin, which only the elite could read.

John Wycliffe, a leading theologian and philosopher at the University of Oxford in England, was increasingly distressed that people had little access to the Scriptures. After much prayer and thought, he decided he needed to do something about it. Christian historian Donald L. Roberts describes Wycliffe's journey this way: "It was not until the twilight of his career that he came to a fully developed position on the authority of the Scriptures. He declared the right of every Christian to know the Bible."[1]

At great risk to his career, Wycliffe began translating the Bible into English. Because of his very vocal beliefs, his reputation was damaged and many of his friends deserted him. He was eventually placed under house arrest, and the pope demanded that he appear in Rome to be tried. Because Wycliffe's health was so poor, he was never forced to make that trip. Instead he used the time he served under house arrest to diligently work on his English translation of the Bible. He saw it completed before he died. And those who supported his work kept alive his English Bible translation and passed it on to the next generation—even in the face of persecution and death.

Forty years after Wycliffe's death, religious authorities tried to silence his influence by digging up his bones, burning them, and scattering the ashes over the River Swift. But they were too late to stop the impact of the translator's work. Wycliffe's commitment to the Scriptures and his English translation ignited a firestorm over Europe in the next several hundred years. Today he is considered "the Morning Star of the Reformation."

The Very Words of God

What would make a scholar like Wycliffe stake everything—even his life—on the authority of the Bible? Because the Bible claims to be the very words of God, and therefore its importance is linked to the character of our heavenly Father. That makes the Bible the most important book in all of history.

The Bible claims that every one of its pages is inspired by God. The apostle Paul writes, "All Scripture is God-breathed and is useful for teaching, rebuking, correcting and training in righteousness" (2 Timothy 3:16 NIV). The picture we get in this verse is of God's Spirit breathing the exact words into the minds of holy people such as the prophets Moses, Isaiah, and Daniel or the apostles Paul, Peter, and John, who then wrote down the words.

God used different methods of imparting His words to the biblical writers, but He always used people who were directed by the Holy Spirit. In some instances biblical writers indicated the supernatural way God directed them. Such was the case for the apostle John, who said this about how he received the instructions to write down the book of Revelation: "It was the Lord's Day, and I was worshiping in the Spirit. Suddenly, I heard behind me a loud voice like a trumpet blast. It said, 'Write in a book everything you see'" (Revelation 1:10-11). The book of Exodus describes how God passed on the Jewish Law, including the

Ten Commandments, to Moses. You can read that miraculous story in Exodus 19:1–20:21. An interesting verse in a later chapter of Exodus also explains how Moses received the Ten Commandments: "When the LORD finished speaking with Moses on Mount Sinai, he gave him the two stone tablets inscribed with the terms of the covenant, written by the finger of God" (Exodus 31:18).

All through the Bible, the text is clear about who its author is. We read phrases like "Word of God," "Word of Truth," and "Word of the Lord." In the Old Testament we see clear evidence that God spoke to the writers. For example, Leviticus 1:1-2, Numbers 1:1, and Deuteronomy 31:24-26 indicate that God spoke to Moses, who wrote down the Books of the Law.

One astounding aspect of God's authorship is that He used humans, writing in their own style. Yet the whole of Scripture—written over thousands of years—is unified and complete. That has to be a miracle of God.

The Words of the Bible

Knowing how God inspired people to write the Bible is essential to recognizing the reliability of the Bible. If God wrote the words, then we must believe them.

Theologians use the term *verbal plenary* inspiration to describe the fact that God "moved along" the writers to produce Scripture. Verbal plenary inspiration insists that God moved people to record not only His *thoughts* but also the actual *words* of Scripture, all the while allowing the writers to express their unique personalities and writing techniques.

Anglican Bible scholar J.C. Ryle writes, "I do maintain that all parts of the Bible are equally 'given by inspiration of God,' and that they are to be regarded as God's Word...The least verse in the Bible is just as truly 'given by inspiration' as the greatest."[2]

Verbal plenary inspiration means that the Bible is fully inspired, not just in part but in *all* its parts. This makes it impossible for anyone to say that the Bible is not fully the Word of God. We may also be sure that the Word of God is found *only* in the Bible and in no other book. The Bible accurately reveals both God's thoughts and words to us. From beginning to end and in all its parts, the Bible is the written Word of God.

This means that the Bible in all its parts is a *spirit-imbued* book. Scripture is not only a *form* of writing produced by the Spirit but also a *forum* where we encounter the Spirit. This reality is seen in the connection between *word* and *spirit* throughout the Bible. For example, Jesus said, "The Spirit alone gives eternal life. Human effort accomplishes nothing. And the very words I have spoken to you are spirit and life" (John 6:63). Note that Jesus's words, as recorded in Scripture, are not just *produced by* the Spirit but *are* "spirit."

Our Confidence in the Author

We can be confident of the reliability of Scripture because we can be confident of its author.

1. God's nature is eternal. The author determines the tone of the book. An autobiography written by a Hollywood celebrity will reflect that person's values and beliefs about a variety of issues. The viewpoints expressed in that book will probably differ significantly from the perspectives expressed in an autobiography of a missionary or that of a Marxist dictator. The Bible—God's autobiography—expresses His viewpoint, one that is so far above our human limitations that we can't even imagine all that He knows. When Job questioned God's wisdom, God answered him out of a storm:

> "Where were you when I laid the foundations of the earth?
>   Tell me, if you know so much.
> Who determined its dimensions
>   and stretched out the surveying line?
> What supports its foundations,
>   and who laid its cornerstone
> as the morning stars sang together
>   and all the angels shouted for joy?"
>   (Job 38:4-7)

The answer to these rhetorical questions is: Only God has existed forever. He is eternal, all-powerful, and all-knowing. And He has put His wisdom and knowledge into His autobiography. His words are perfectly true and righteous because God's nature is truth and righteousness.

2. God backs up what He says. Years ago when my father was raising his family in Coweta, Oklahoma, he considered his word his bond. When he made a promise or proposed an oral contract and shook on the deal, he wouldn't break his word. Most of the people who lived in that area during his day also followed this practice.

When God makes a contract, He *always* keeps it. Sometimes circumstances arise that cause us to break our word. A businessperson agrees to financial terms but then has an unforeseen business failure. A homeowner signs a house loan but then later suffers a debilitating illness that sends him into bankruptcy. But God, who has all power and all knowledge, is able to fulfill all His contracts.

This is what Jesus said about the finality of God's words: "I tell you the truth, until heaven and earth disappear, not even the smallest detail of God's law will disappear until its purpose is achieved" (Matthew 5:18). A verse from the Old Testament emphasizes the same truth: "I am the Lord! If I say it, it will happen" (Ezekiel 12:25).

Therefore, we go to God's Word to find out what God says about the past, present, and future. This helps us understand history, our present lives, and our future. God's Word assures us of what God has done, is doing, and will do for us as we obey Him.

3. God and His Word are perfect. What kind of a standard did God set for His Word? Perfection. Every detail, every thought, and every moment of historical reference in its pages are completely right. In fact, their surety goes beyond this universe.

> Your eternal word, O Lord,
>   stands firm in heaven.
>   (Psalm 119:89)

The reason God's Word can last forever is because it is perfect. It is like a building that is erected on a good foundation. Any contractor will tell you that if the foundation of a multistory building is laid even a fraction of an inch off on any side, the error will multiply itself as the building rises. But if the foundation is laid perfectly true, the rest of the building is solid. Because God's Word is a perfect foundation for life, anything we build on it will be solid and secure. Psalm 19:7-8 says,

> The instructions of the LORD are perfect,
>   reviving the soul.
> The decrees of the LORD are trustworthy,
>   making wise the simple.
> The commandments of the LORD are right,
>   bringing joy to the heart.
> The commands of the LORD are clear,
>   giving insight for living.

God and His Word are perfect for every aspect of life.

What Does the Bible Teach Us?

The Bible is God's way of communicating with us. Through the dialogue God gives us in His Word, we learn two things—what God is like and what we are like.

We Gain a View of God

Historian David McCullough's book *John Adams* was a *New York Times* best-seller. For most people, John Adams, the second American president, is little more than a name on a list. His life was overshadowed by that of George Washington. But McCullough shows what an astounding influence John Adams had on the early days of our nation. Adams was a "devout Christian and an independent thinker." Although he came from an undistinguished background, he "emerged as one of the most 'sensible and forcible' figures in the whole patriot cause."[3] After reading the book, you will gain a deeper understanding of the godly character and the trustworthy nature of this man who so influenced our nation. But until you do, you will never understand the contribution he made to our way of life.

In some ways we could call the Bible the autobiography of God. Of course, no one can truly describe God's infinite character in a book—or even in human language. But God has chosen to use words that help us glimpse His majesty and love. We can see His glory in every situation in the Bible. Therefore, if we want to know what God is like, we will read His autobiography. Reading the Bible will give us more insight into His nature than anything else we can do.

We Gain a More Accurate View of Ourselves

The *Peanuts* character Pig Pen makes us chuckle. He walks along in a cloud of dust, happy just the way he is. Doesn't this remind you of many little boys? They play outside in the dirt and come in with half the yard on their bodies. But if their mothers ask them if they need to take a bath, they respond, "I'm not that dirty. All I need to do is wash my hands."

We laugh at children's oblivion to their own state of uncleanness, but we are similar to them in one way. We are spiritually dirty, full of wrongdoing and sin, yet we don't even recognize how desperately we need cleansing. The Bible shows us who we are: "For the word of God is alive and powerful. It is sharper than the sharpest two-edged sword, cutting between soul and spirit, between joint and marrow. It exposes our innermost thoughts and desires. Nothing in all creation is hidden from God. Everything is naked and exposed before his eyes, and he is the one to whom we are accountable" (Hebrews 4:12-13).

Not only does the Bible expose our sin, but it also explains who we are in Christ. Consider these perspectives and promises:

> The law was our guardian until Christ came; it protected us until we could be made right with God through faith (Galatians 3:24).

> Even before he made the world, God loved us and chose us in Christ to be holy and without fault in his eyes (Ephesians 1:4).

We are God's masterpiece. He has created us anew in Christ Jesus, so we can do the good things he planned for us long ago (Ephesians 2:10).

For I can do everything through Christ, who gives me strength (Philippians 4:13).

And the Bible shows us our future. The apostle Peter writes, "All praise to God, the Father of our Lord Jesus Christ. It is by his great mercy that we have been born again, because God raised Jesus Christ from the dead. Now we live with great expectation, and we have a priceless inheritance—an inheritance that is kept in heaven for you, pure and undefiled, beyond the reach of change and decay" (1 Peter 1:3-4).

Discovering Our God

Getting to know God through His Word is one of the most satisfying and marvelous opportunities of my lifetime. As I get to know God better, I also understand my own weaknesses more fully and how I can, through God's power, become more like God's Son, Jesus Christ. The more Christlike I become, the more I please my heavenly Father.

To help you begin the journey to knowing God better, I have included in the Discover the Treasure section a study on the names of God. Knowing what God calls Himself gives us great insight into His personality. As you look up these names, you will also become more acquainted with the layout of the books of the Bible. Use the contents page in the front of your Bible to help you locate books that may be hard for you to find.

The next chapter will continue our discussion on why the Bible is so important by addressing its reliability. We will discover that God has given us many proofs of the trustworthiness of His Word.

DISCOVER THE TREASURE

In Bible times, a person's name often gave insight into his or her role in life. For example, God changed Abram's name to Abraham, which means "father of many," because he would be the physical ancestor of the Jewish nation and the spiritual ancestor of all who truly believe in God (see Genesis 17:1-8). In the New Testament, Saul changed his name to Paul after his conversion and his decision to serve as an evangelist. He had been transformed from a murderer to a life-changer.

We can be sure that the names God calls Himself reflect what He wants us to know about Him. One of the names that is most common throughout the Bible is Father. What a wonderful picture that gives us of His loving care for us, His people.

As you go through each of these verses, look them up and write down what the name means to you. Then take a moment to praise God for this magnificent quality. The first one is done for you as an example. You may want to use a few of the following exercises as part of your quiet time with God for the next few days.

Father—God our heavenly Father (Deuteronomy 32:6; Matthew 6:9)
What this means to me:
I can entrust my life to His care.

Adonai—"Lord" or "Master" (Psalm 39:7; Luke 6:46)
What this means to me:

El-Elyon—"Exalted One," "the Most High" (Numbers 24:16)
What this means to me:

El-Roi—"the God who sees" (Psalm 139:1-2,7)

What this means to me:

El-Olam—"Eternal God" (Habakkuk 3:6)

What this means to me:

Immanuel—"God with us" (Matthew 1:23)

What this means to me:

Jehovah—"I AM" (Exodus 3:14-15)

What this means to me:

Jehovah-Rohi—"the Lord our Shepherd" (Isaiah 40:11; John 10:11)

What this means to me:

Jehovah-Rapha—"God our Healer" (Exodus 15:26; Luke 4:18)

What this means to me:

Jehovah-Shalom—"God our Peace" (Isaiah 9:6; John 16:33)

What this means to me:

2

Is the Bible Trustworthy?

Do you accept the Bible as absolute truth? Do you know the peace and blessing that comes from living out its supernatural, life-transforming message?

The year I left Princeton Theological Seminary to continue my studies at Fuller Theological Seminary, I had the opportunity to hear two very gifted young evangelists during our chapel program. Both believed and preached the Word of God as God's inspired truth.

Later, however, both began to question whether the Bible was truly inspired in every way and in every word. One of these men rejected the integrity of God's Word. As a result, he had no moorings on which to base his life and ministry. He got a divorce, left the ministry, and eventually became an outspoken antagonist of the Christian faith. The other young man chose to believe that the Bible was truly the Word of God. Even what he could not understand at first, he entrusted to God until he could understand it.

I won't mention the name of the first man, but the second man is my longtime friend Billy Graham, whom God has used to touch the lives of millions of people around the world. Certainly not every preacher can expect to have an impact on the world the way Billy Graham has, but embracing the Bible as perfect always goes hand in hand with dynamic and effective preaching.

The most important thing I learned throughout my long life, other than the blessing of knowing Christ personally, is that the Bible is truly God's Word. It can be trusted implicitly. In seminary I learned that I could have absolute, unshakable confidence in the authority of God's holy, inspired Word. It is the anchor of my soul. Through the years, I have observed that when people are faced with the great challenges of heartache, sorrow, testing, and trials, the only thing that provides real confidence and hope is the holy, inspired Word of God. There is no other anchor that compares to God's Word.

In this chapter and the next, we'll examine the supernatural nature of the Bible, how every word contained within its pages is Holy Spirit inspired, fully true, and worthy of your trust. God gives us many proofs that the Bible is reliable. Some come from the text of the Bible itself, others from church history, science, and archaeology.

True and Trustworthy

Inseparably linked to the doctrine of the inspiration of Scripture are two other biblical doctrines: biblical inerrancy and biblical infallibility. The first teaches that the Bible is absolutely *true;* the second flows from this premise and affirms the Bible to be absolutely *trustworthy.*

You will not find the word *inerrancy* in the Bible. But like the doctrine of the Trinity, it is a truth nevertheless taught in Scripture. The crucial doctrine of inerrancy teaches that the Bible is absolutely *true,* without error. The psalmist wrote:

> All your words are true;
>> all your righteous laws are eternal.
>> (Psalm 119:160 NIV)

In the New Testament, John writes, "Sanctify them by the truth; your word is truth" (John 17:17 NIV). Jesus declares the enduring truth of biblical law when he says, "Heaven and earth will disappear, but my words will never disappear" (Luke 21:33). The writer of Hebrews affirmed the reliability of the God who is always truthful: "So God has given both his promise and his oath. These two things are unchangeable because it is impossible for God to lie. Therefore, we who have fled to him for refuge can have great confidence as we hold to the hope that lies before us" (Hebrews 6:18). We see from these select

Scriptures that every single word of the Bible is completely accurate and trustworthy.

The Proof from Prophecy

The reliability of the Bible is seen in the amazing fulfillment of Old Testament prophecy in the New Testament. It is one undeniable proof that the Bible can stand the test of time. It has been 100 percent accurate.

Modern clairvoyants Jeanne Dixon and Edgar Cayce once tantalized many Americans with the thought that their futures could be predicted with a large measure of accuracy. Today, psychics claiming to forecast your future and calm your fears about tomorrow are available over the phone for a few dollars a minute. The problem, however, is that although psychics, mediums, and spiritists boast of remarkable predictions, they are often wrong. Jeanne Dixon predicted that Richard Nixon would win the 1960 presidential election, but John F. Kennedy did. And she also predicted that Russia would beat the United States to the moon.

According to the Old Testament, a prophet who speaks for God must be 100 percent accurate. The Bible records the acid test for a prophet: "But you may wonder, 'How will we know whether or not a prophecy is from the LORD?' If the prophet speaks in the LORD's name but his prediction does not happen or come true, you will know that the LORD did not give that message. That prophet has spoken without my authority and need not be feared" (Deuteronomy 18:21-22). What becomes of prophets if they are ever wrong? They are to die (see Deuteronomy 18:20).

Scholars estimate we can find approximately twenty-five hundred prophecies in the Bible. Roughly two thousand of those have been fulfilled with remarkable precision. Because I believe we are living in the last days before Christ's second coming, I look forward to seeing the remaining five hundred come to pass in the near future. But the odds that all two thousand prophecies could have been fulfilled by chance is less than one in 10^{2000} (that is one with two thousand zeros after it). Biblical scholar Charles C. Ryrie has pointed out that, by the law of chance, it would require two hundred billion earths, populated with four billion people each, to come up with one person who could achieve one hundred accurate prophecies without any errors in sequence.[4] But the Bible records not one hundred but nearly twenty-five hundred prophecies.

Let's look at just some of the exciting Old Testament prophecies that are fulfilled in Jesus Christ. Look up each Old Testament verse and compare it to the New Testament fulfillment. Remember that the prophecies were written hundreds of years before their fulfillment.

PROPHECY ABOUT JESUS		
	OT Reference	NT Fulfillment
Born of a virgin	Isaiah 7:14	Luke 1:26,28
His ministry in Galilee	Isaiah 9:1	Matthew 4:12,14-15
Teacher of parables	Psalm 78:2	Matthew 13:34-35
Crucified with thieves	Isaiah 53:12	Matthew 27:38
His resurrection	Psalm 16:10	Acts 2:31
His ascension	Psalm 68:18	Acts 1:9

Can you imagine how people would receive a contemporary book that had this kind of success in predicting events even just one year in the future? People would flock to buy it, and the author would have a cult following. The verses you looked up are just a sampling of all the prophecies that have been fulfilled since the Bible was written. Without a doubt, the Bible passes the test of reliability.

The Unity of the Bible

The Bible would be less than trustworthy if its message wasn't consistent. The miraculous fact about the Bible is that it has one theme from beginning to end—the glory of God through His Son, Jesus Christ.

When I think about the phenomenal unity of the Bible, as it demonstrates itself at every level of scrutiny, I enthusiastically agree with the following statement, which is said to have been found inside a Gideon's Bible:

> This Book is the mind of God, the state of man, the way of salvation, the doom of sinners, and the happiness of believers. Its doctrines are holy, its precepts are binding; its histories are true, and its decisions are immutable. Read it to be wise, believe it to be safe, practice it to be holy. It contains light to direct you, food to support you, and comfort to cheer you. It is the traveler's map, the pilgrim's staff, the pilot's compass, the soldier's sword, and the Christian's character. Here paradise is restored, heaven opened, and the gates of hell disclosed. Christ is its grand subject, our good its design, and the glory of God its end. It should fill the memory, rule the heart, and guide the feet. Read it slowly, frequently, prayerfully. It is a mine of wealth, a paradise of glory, and a river of pleasure. Follow its precepts and it will lead you to Calvary, to the empty tomb, to a resurrected life in Christ; yes, to glory itself, for eternity.[5]

The Bible presents a unified message, not a loose assortment of religious ideas. One amazing example of the Bible's unity is the comparison of the four Gospels—Matthew, Mark, Luke, and John. Each writer presents the life of Christ from a different angle:

Matthew—Jesus as the king

Mark—Jesus as a servant

Luke—Jesus as the perfect man

John—Jesus as the Son of God

These writers describe the same events in the life of Jesus, and even though they emphasize the events in different ways, their accounts all match up.

The rest of the Bible shows the same unity, despite the fact that it consists of sixty-six books written by some forty different authors over a period of fifteen hundred years. The unity of Scripture is one of the clearest indications of its supernatural origin. Only the sovereign God of the universe could have superintended the writing of Scripture so that every line remains in total agreement. The Bible is unquestionably the book that God wrote.

The Indestructibility of the Bible

If you scan the books on your bookshelf, how many of them were written more than twenty-five years ago? How many were written a century ago? How many were written a millennium ago? Truthfully, most books written today have a marketability of only a few short years.

The Bible has a different track record. Perhaps the earliest book in the Bible is Job. Although Bible historians cannot be sure of the date of the writing of the book, they believe Job lived around the time of Abraham. Job's lifespan probably occurred around four thousand years ago. The account may have been penned thirty-five hundred years ago. The Bible truly has lasted longer than any other book.

What's amazing about this record is that the Bible has survived in spite of tremendous persecution through the years. Arthur W. Pink, a Bible historian, writes:

> When we bear in mind the fact that the Bible has been the special object of never ending persecution the *wonder* of the Bible's survival is changed into a *miracle*...For two thousand years man's hatred of the Bible has been persistent, determined, relentless, and murderous. Every possible effort has been made to undermine faith in the inspiration and authority of the Bible, and innumerable enterprises have been undertaken to consign it to oblivion. Imperial edicts have been issued to the effect that every known copy of the Bible should be destroyed, and when this measure failed to exterminate and annihilate God's Word, then commands were given that every person found with a copy of the Scriptures in his possession should be put to death. The very fact that the Bible has been so singled out for such relentless persecution causes us to wonder at such a unique phenomenon.[6]

An interesting story about this persecution involves the Roman emperor Diocletian. In a royal edict proclaimed in AD 303, he demanded that every copy of the Bible be burned. Theologian Henry Thiessen describes the incredible results:

> He had killed so many Christians and destroyed so many Bibles, that when the Christians remained silent for a season and kept in hiding, he thought that he had actually put an end to the Scriptures. He caused a medal to be struck with the inscription: "The Christian religion is destroyed and the worship of the [Roman] gods restored." But it was only a few years later that Constantine came to the throne and that he made Christianity the state religion. What would Diocletian say if he could return to earth and see how the Bible has gone on in its world mission?[7]

The Bible Text

Another aspect of the Bible's indestructibility is that the Bible we read today is a translation from texts that have not changed in thousands of years. Before the printing press was invented, the text of the Bible was copied by hand. The scribes who did the copying received special training. Some dedicated their entire lives to this task. They were so careful about what they did that after four thousand years scholars can find only a handful of discrepancies between the earliest Hebrew manuscripts and today's Hebrew texts. Through these scribes and other events, God has preserved His Word through the centuries.

One of the most important factors supporting the accuracy of the Old Testament is the discovery of the Dead Sea Scrolls, which date from 200 BC to AD 68. In 1947, a Bedouin shepherd boy was traveling the northwest rim of the Dead Sea when he discovered a jar in a cave containing scrolls that had been hidden for nearly two thousand years. The term *Dead Sea Scrolls* became the standard designation for the fragmentary manuscripts discovered in the limestone caves around the Dead Sea. To the astonishment of biblical archaeologists, all the books of the Bible except the book of Esther are represented in the collection. Comparison with Old Testament manuscripts of a thousand years later shows little or no variation between them.

Contained in the manuscripts was a copy of the oldest known Hebrew manuscript of the book of Isaiah. Strikingly, the document is extremely similar to the book of Isaiah found in today's Bibles.

During his lifetime, Yale University professor Millar Burrows was one the world's most respected biblical archaeologists. Regarding the book of Isaiah discovered near the Dead Sea, he observes,

> Of the 166 *words* in Isaiah 53, there are only seventeen *letters* in question. Ten of these letters are simply a matter of spelling, which does not affect the sense. Four more letters are minor stylistic changes, such as conjunctions. The remaining three letters comprise the word, "light," which is added in verse 11, and does not affect the meaning greatly. Furthermore, this word is supported by the LXX and IQ Is (one of the Isaiah scrolls found in the Dead Sea caves). Thus, in one chapter of 166 words, there is only one word (three letters) in question after a thousand years of transmission—and this word does not significantly change the meaning of the passage.[8]

Dr. Burrows concludes, "It is a matter of wonder that through something like a thousand years the text underwent so little alteration."[9] The discovery of the Dead Sea Scrolls thoroughly discredits the charge that the original Old Testament has been lost because of numerous copies and translations. God certainly has protected His Word—for our benefit.

The Testimony from Church History

We can also go to sources outside the biblical text to prove its reliability. In addition to the Bible's own claims, the early church fathers also supported the inerrancy of Scripture. The early church fathers are significant because many people consider them to be the successors to the original apostles of Jesus.

Clement of Rome (AD 30–96), the third bishop of Rome and close associate of the apostle Paul (see Philippians 4:3), believed that the Scriptures were given through the Holy Spirit. Saint Augustine (AD 354–430), considered to be one of the most outstanding theologians in all of church history, believed in the inspiration and inerrancy of Scripture. Saint Gregory the Great (AD 540–604), known for his great influence on shaping the doctrine, organization, and rules of discipline of the early church, wrote: "Most superfluous it is to inquire who wrote these things. We loyally believe the Holy Ghost to be the Author of the Book. He wrote it Who dictated it for writing; He wrote it Who inspired its execution."[10]

The testimony of Scripture and the testimony of biblical scholars throughout the centuries is clear: The Bible is indeed reliable. The Bible is true because God is truth and cannot lie (see John 7:28). As a result, His Word is truth (see John 17:17). Now let us see how science affirms the Bible's trustworthiness.

Proof from Science

Although the Bible is not a scientific manual, when it mentions scientific facts, it is accurate. Sometimes these facts have not been proven true until centuries after they were written.

In the "Science" section of its March 5, 1990, issue, *Time* magazine had an item, "Score One for the Bible," refuting the research of the late British archaeologist Kathleen Kenyon, who claimed that Jericho was destroyed 150 years before the Bible records the Israelites' destruction of the city. *Time* also noted many facts consistent with the biblical story.[11] While Bible believers certainly do not need scientific proof as a prop for their faith, it is always nice when science and periodicals like *Time* catch up with the Word of God. Here are a few of the scientific truths found in the Bible:

- Many centuries before Galileo (1564–1642) claimed that the earth was round, the Bible declared, "God sits above the circle of the earth. The people below seem like grasshoppers to him!" (Isaiah 40:22).

- Matthew Maury (1806–1873) is considered the father of oceanography. When he was bedridden during a serious illness, he asked his son to read to him from the Bible.

While listening to Psalm 8:8 in the King James Version, Maury noticed the expression "paths of the seas." Upon his recovery, Maury went looking for these paths, and as a result, discovered the continental currents. Maury's book on oceanography is still considered a basic text on the subject and continues to be used in many universities.

- A Roman engineer named Marcus Vitruvius discovered the hydrologic water cycle in 30 BC. Yet this truth was fully revealed to mankind in 1600 BC. The Bible records, "Rivers run into the sea, but the sea is never full. Then the water returns again to the rivers and flows out again to the sea" (Ecclesiastes 1:7).

- The earth's gravitational field is mentioned in Scripture: "God stretches the northern sky over empty space and hangs the earth on nothing" (Job 26:7).

Because science supports the claims of the Bible, it is no wonder that many of the world's great scientists were Christians who looked to Scripture as the foundation for their knowledge of the universe. Examples include Nicolaus Copernicus, Johannes Kepler, Galileo Galilei, Robert Boyle, George Washington Carver, Michael Faraday, Samuel Morse, Isaac Newton, Gregor Mendel, Louis Pasteur, and the Wright brothers.

Proof from Archaeology

For centuries skeptics have claimed that the Bible is filled with historical errors. They have pointed to several biblical accounts, particularly in the Old Testament, where archaeology contradicted the Bible. So what has happened over the years? In many cases scientists have been proven to be inaccurate and the Bible has been shown to be trustworthy and reliable. Here are a few examples:

- Scientists stated that the Bible is historically inaccurate because they believed that King David was a fictional

character. They said that the remains of Egyptian, Babylonian, and Assyrian cultures make no specific reference
to him. But a group of archaeologists found in northern
Israel an Assyrian stone tablet dating from the ninth century BC. It shows an Aramaic inscription listing Assyria's
enemies. Included in the list were the words "king of Israel"
and "house of David."[12]

- The most documented biblical event is the worldwide
  flood described in Genesis 6–9. Discoveries indicate that
  a number of Babylonian documents describe the same
  flood. "The Sumerian King List...for example, lists kings
  who reigned for long periods of time. Then a great flood
  came. Following the flood, Sumerian kings ruled for much
  shorter periods of time. This is the same pattern found in
  the Bible. People had long life spans before the flood and
  shorter life spans after the flood. Also, the 11th tablet of
  the Gilgamesh Epic speaks of an ark, animals taken on the
  ark, birds sent out during the course of the flood, the ark
  landing on a mountain, and a sacrifice offered after the ark
  landed."[13]

- "The discovery of the Ebla archive in northern Syria in
  the 1970s has shown the biblical writings about the Patri-
  archs to be viable. Documents written on clay tablets from
  around 2300 B.C. demonstrate that the personal names in
  the Patriarchal accounts are genuine."[14]

- "The Hittites were once thought to be a biblical legend,
  until their capital and records were discovered at Bogazkoy,
  Turkey."[15]

- "It was once claimed there was no Assyrian king named
  Sargon as recorded in Isaiah 20:1, because this name was
  not known in any other record. Then, Sargon's palace was
  discovered in Khorsabad, Iraq. The very event mentioned
  in Isaiah 20, his capture of Ashdod, was recorded on the

palace walls. What is more, fragments of a stela memorial-
izing the victory were found at Ashdod itself."[16]

- "Another king who was in doubt was Belshazzar, king of
  Babylon, named in Daniel 5. The last king of Babylon was
  Nabonidus according to recorded history. Tablets were
  found showing that Belshazzar was Nabonidus' son who
  served as coregent in Babylon. Thus, Belshazzar could offer
  to make Daniel 'third highest ruler in the kingdom' (Dan.
  5:16) for reading the handwriting on the wall, the highest
  available position."[17]

The Bible Is Our Guide

These are just some of the amazing scientific and archaeological
facts contained in the Bible, facts now supported by prominent scientists. But why should anyone be surprised that the book that *is* truth
would *contain* truth on these and many other subjects? The Bible has
been proven to be reliable. No one has proven otherwise. If the Bible
is reliable, then its words are true.

When we let God's Word be the standard for our lives, we won't be
swayed by the world's reasoning or our own feelings. We can always
search for the right way to think and act.

That's why it is so vital to understand the central message of the
Bible. We can believe that the Bible is reliable, but until we know what
it says, its trustworthiness will do us no good. If we do not allow the
Bible to center our viewpoint, we will wander off course.

One way we can allow the Bible to guide our lives is to hide the
Word in our hearts. Whenever we get into a situation in which we are
tempted to do wrong or we don't know quite what God would want us
to do, the Holy Spirit can bring an appropriate memorized passage to
our mind. Then we can let God's Word guide us in that situation. Or
if we are in a crisis and need encouragement, help with fear, or strength
of purpose, those verses we have learned will aid us. In our Discover
the Treasure section, I show you how you can take just a few minutes
of your day to memorize Scripture. I encourage you to begin a plan to

hide God's Word in your heart and see what God will do to bless you through His Word.

DISCOVER THE TREASURE

Whenever many adults hear the word *memorize,* they groan, "I could never do that." Yet all of us memorize many things in our daily lives: telephone numbers, passwords, account numbers, addresses, commercial jingles, sayings by famous people. You have much more capacity to memorize than you realize.

We should memorize Scripture, if for no other reason than the Lord commanded us to learn His Word (see Proverbs 7:1-3). When you have stored Bible promises in your heart and mind, you will soon notice other changes in your life because the Holy Spirit will use the verses to teach you new things and to help you resist temptation (see Psalm 119:11).

As a new believer, I memorized many verses. The verse 1 Corinthians 10:13 alone—"The temptations in your life are no different from what others experience. And God is faithful. He will not allow the temptation to be more than you can stand. When you are tempted, he will show you a way out so that you can endure"—has saved me from disobeying God on hundreds, if not thousands, of occasions. As we memorize God's Word, the verses become part of the inner workings of our mind, and the Holy Spirit uses them to guide us through situations we encounter during our day.

If you develop a systematic method, Scripture memory will take just a few minutes a day. Look for small slots of time that you normally waste and fill them with memorizing God's Word. Instead of reading a magazine in the doctor's office, memorize a verse of Scripture. Use your break at work, or arrange to memorize Scripture with a fellow believer from your workplace, campus, or church. Memorize Scripture as a family. Memorize verses that you find in your quiet time with God or that you hear in a sermon. Memorizing verses that apply to your daily life will be easier since you will use them as you memorize them.

Reviewing what you have memorized is just as important as the initial memorization stage. Here are some suggestions for organizing your review.

- Write your memory verses on index cards and carry them with you to review whenever you have a few free moments.

- Use a pocket-size notebook to write your verses and the dates you learned them. Review your list often.

- Build a chart of key verses that God has used in your life. Review them as you thank Him for how He has worked in your life.

- Keep a list of key verses from your personal or small-group Bible study. Memorize those verses to make your study more meaningful. Review them periodically.

- Post index cards with verses in places where you need them most. For example, tape a card with Philippians 4:8—"Fix your thoughts on what is true, and honorable, and right, and pure, and lovely, and admirable. Think about things that are excellent and worthy of praise"—above your television set.

Here is a list of some verses you could use to begin your memorization:

The power of memorizing God's Word:

> I have hidden your word in my heart,
> that I might not sin against you.
> (Psalm 119:11)

The gospel in a nutshell:

> "For this is how God loved the world: He gave his one and only Son, so that everyone who believes in him will not perish but have eternal life" (John 3:16).

How to seek God's will:

> Trust in the LORD with all your heart;
>> do not depend on your own understanding.
> Seek his will in all you do,
>> and he will show you which path to take.
>> (Proverbs 3:5-6)

How to resist temptation:

> The temptations in your life are no different from what others experience. And God is faithful. He will not allow the temptation to be more than you can stand. When you are tempted, he will show you a way out so that you can endure (1 Corinthians 10:13).

What to think about:

> And now, dear brothers and sisters, one final thing. Fix your thoughts on what is true, and honorable, and right, and pure, and lovely, and admirable. Think about things that are excellent and worthy of praise (Philippians 4:8).

The Great Commandment:

> "So now I am giving you a new commandment: Love each other. Just as I have loved you, you should love each other. Your love for one another will prove to the world that you are my disciples" (John 13:34-35).

The Great Commission:

> Jesus came and told his disciples, "I have been given all authority in heaven and on earth. Therefore, go and make disciples of all the nations, baptizing them in the name of the Father and the Son and the Holy Spirit. Teach these new disciples to obey all the commands I have given you. And be sure of this: I am with you always, even to the end of the age" (Matthew 28:18-20).

3

What Is the Bible's Message?

When the former Soviet Union opened up to the gospel as the Communist government collapsed, I met with one of the most influential generals in the Russian military. I had the incredible joy of giving him a Bible.

He took the book with a sense of awe. He said slowly, "I have never had a Bible before. This is the first Bible I have ever held in my hand." Can you imagine this commanding general, in the prime of his career, staring in wonder as he actually held God's Word in his hands?

In American culture we take the Bible too lightly. Perhaps this is because we have always had access to the Bible, so we don't realize how supernatural it is. Instead, many people put their Bible on a shelf, and it gathers dust. Although the majority of homes in the United States have a Bible somewhere, most people don't read it or study it. As a result, most people in our country don't know what's in the Bible. According to the Barna Research Group:

- A full 12 percent of adults believe that the name of Noah's wife was Joan of Arc. (The Bible does not provide her name.)

- One out of six people believes that one of the books in the New Testament is the book of Thomas, written by the apostle Thomas. Another one-third of the population is not sure whether there is such a book in the New Testament.

- Half of all adults believe the Bible teaches that money is the root of all evil. One-third (37 percent) disagrees with this contention. The actual teaching indicates that "the love of money is the root of all kinds of evil" (1 Timothy 6:10).[18]

Tragically, those who fail to embrace the Scriptures as the supreme guide for their lives are people who wander in the dark without a light to direct their steps. They are destined to live aimless and unproductive lives. They have no firm foundation but rather drift from one whim of culture to the next.

When we neglect or ignore the message of God's Word, we do so to our detriment. In it is the revelation of God's Word to mankind. Here is found not only the foundation for absolute truth but also absolute truth itself. While for thousands of years empty philosophies have risen and then faded from sight, the Bible continues to shine like a beacon in the dark night, lighting the way for all who would follow it to safety. Ask people who walk in its precepts and councils, and they will share that walking the path of God's Word does not lead to hopelessness and despair but to a life of redemption, joy, and blessing.

Words Empowered by the Spirit

A close friend of mine attended a seminar led by a theologian who didn't believe in the inerrancy of Scripture. The speaker began his talk about Bible interpretation with a discussion on the nature and authority of the Bible. Even though the speaker knew of my friend's reputation as an evangelical believer, committed to the Bible as divinely inspired, this self-avowed skeptic criticized the Bible as an antiquated document with not a shred of divine inspiration attached to it. He believed that the Bible contained errors and fallacies.

Suddenly, in front of the entire group, my friend walked over to the speaker, opened up a copy of the Bible, and said, "The Holy Spirit lives within this book."

"On what page of the Bible does the Holy Spirit live?" the theologian asked.

My friend thought for a moment, then responded, "In each and every page; in each and every word." He then quoted Jesus, "The Spirit alone gives eternal life. Human effort accomplishes nothing. And the very *words* I have spoken to you *are spirit* and life. But some of you do not believe me" (John 6:63-64, emphasis added).

The speaker looked back with a blank stare.

The truth the speaker missed is that the pages of the Bible are effective only because the message they contain is of the Spirit. He is the one who formed the Bible to contain one clear message. It is only through His power and wisdom that the Bible is so supernaturally consistent. Let's look at several truths regarding the focus and message of the Bible.

The Message Is Uniform

The Bible presents a uniform message, which means that no biblical writer ever introduced new truth. For example, Isaiah did not introduce any spiritual concepts that were not already revealed by Moses. James did not add to Peter any more than Peter added to Paul. Rather, each successive biblical writer developed, or brought to light, certain aspects of truth that previously existed in seed form. This means that the Bible does not contain sixty-six *individual* books, but sixty-six *stages* in the development of one, unified message. This fact is a result of the sovereign guidance of the Holy Spirit—not human brilliance.

The image of the seed helps us understand the unified nature of the Bible. When a seed from a pinecone falls to the ground and begins to sprout, every facet of life related to the growth and development of the new tree is present within that seed. Over time, a defined root system emerges, which produces a trunk, resulting in branches, which in turn produce pinecones with more seeds.

When God revealed His holy Word to Moses in the Old Testament book of Genesis, the seed of God's divine revelation to mankind was planted. Like the pine seed that bears all the qualities of the tree, *every spiritual truth contained in the Bible is first established in Genesis.*

For example, in the first three chapters of Genesis alone we find the grand doctrine of creation (1:1-31), the doctrine of the Cultural Mandate (1:28), the doctrine of natural revelation (chapter 1), principles of marriage (2:18-25), the doctrine of sin (3:6-7), the doctrine of redemption (3:15), the doctrine of covenant (2:15-17), the principle of temptation (3:1), the principle of life (2:7), the principle of good and evil (2:9), the principle of death (2:17), the doctrine of the Word (1:3), and the principle of judgment (3:8-24). Isn't that amazing?

From the Old Testament book of Exodus forward, God unlocks and develops these truths and many others. He does this through successive redemptive acts, covenants, and teachings—which all bring to light the hidden aspects of the plan of redemption. This gradual development forms the trunk and the branches of revelation. This pattern is clearly seen in the unfolding from one book to the next. And it is most evident in the relationship the Old Testament bears to the New Testament. My friend Bruce Wilkinson, founder of the Walk Thru the Bible ministry, explains this so well:

> God chose to reveal Himself in a progressive way, and His written Word gradually unfolded more and more truth about His person and work. It has been said that the New [Testament] is in the Old [Testament] concealed, and the Old is in the New revealed. The thirty-nine books of the Old Testament provide the foundation upon which the superstructure of the twenty-seven books of the New Testament is built.[19]

With this fact before us, we see ever more clearly that the Bible is a body of truth that is interrelated and interdependent. Just as you cannot understand the functions of your hand in isolation from the way your whole body works, so the New Testament cannot be grasped apart from the Old Testament, and the Pauline Epistles cannot be properly understood without knowledge of the four Gospels, and so it goes.

The Writers Agree

The biblical writers' message agrees, despite their varied historical, social, linguistic, and stylistic differences. The wonder of this miracle of the Spirit is that all this was done over a period of hundreds of years through many writers. As previously mentioned, the Bible consists of sixty-six books written by some forty different authors over a period of 1500 years. The first writer, Moses, died about 1450 years before the last writer, John, was even born. Yet not one writer ever denounced the teachings of another or taught anything that could be considered contradictory of the other writers of Scripture. Their message remains consistent throughout.

Think about that. As of this writing I am eighty-one years old. In that time the worldwide church has witnessed the birth of thousands of new spiritual movements, all claiming to represent God's will and ways. In many cases, the leaders of these movements felt compelled to criticize the teachings of other religious groups to legitimize their own beliefs. Many religious leaders don't even agree to the same foundational message. What are the odds that some forty different spiritual leaders, writing over a period of 1500 years, and all claiming divine guidance, could remain in total agreement? The spiritual and doctrinal oneness of the biblical writers, despite their diverse historical settings, proves once again that the Bible derives from one divine mind.

Different social standing. The Bible's message is consistent despite the differences in the writers' social standing. The writers of the Bible included kings, farmers, shepherds, scholars, commoners, and priests. One was a physician, and others were fishermen. What an incredibly diverse group. Yet these people, from assorted walks of life and spread over many years, remained in total accord on every doctrine they addressed.

Different languages. The Bible's message is consistent despite the diversity of the languages employed by the writers. The Bible was written in three different languages—Hebrew, Aramaic, and Greek. Imagine what would happen if you asked forty authors, representing three different languages, to write a chapter about God with the instruction that they are not to compare their ideas. Their work would then be made into a single book. What a mess we would have. It would very likely be a work full of assorted theories about faith, God, heaven, and more. Certainly, this book's message wouldn't be considered a unit. Yet the Bible presents a consistent system of truth, which is viewed by many millions of people as God's infallible Word. This feat is so miraculous that we can't imagine its depth.

I heard a story about a wealthy woman who, while traveling overseas, saw a bracelet she thought was irresistible. So she sent her husband this cable: "Have found wonderful bracelet. Price $75,000. May I buy it?"

Her husband promptly wired back: "No, price too high."

But the cable operator omitted the comma, so the woman received this message: "No price too high." Elated, she purchased the bracelet.

Needless to say, at her return her husband was dismayed. It was just a little thing, a comma, but what a difference it made. Compare this to the fact that the exact meaning of the Bible's message has been preserved down through the ages and that every part of it harmonizes beautifully. Unquestionably, the Bible is no ordinary book.

Consider this: Genesis, which was written by a nomadic Hebrew named Moses, harmonizes perfectly with the book of Revelation, a book of visions and symbols written in Greek by an imprisoned Christian named John. For example, in Genesis, Satan questions God's Word, but in Revelation, Satan is defeated and God's Word is vindicated before all creation. Whereas in Genesis, the first people forfeit their state of innocence and freedom from suffering through sin, Revelation contains the promise of a new heavens and a new earth where "[God] will wipe every tear from their eyes" (21:4). The languages used by the writers of Genesis and Revelation varied, yet the themes they employed are identical. We have looked at only two examples, but it is worth noting that *every* theological theme that is established in Genesis is recapped in Revelation.

Different writing styles. The unified message of Scripture is also maintained despite the widely different writing styles of the biblical writers. The Bible contains the loftiest poetry and the deepest prose. While one writer incorporates symbolism and imagery, another takes us through sweeping overviews of history. One appeals to our senses with allegories, while another presses our minds with sound arguments sharpened with acute logic. Not only do characteristic expressions and mannerisms differ between each writer, but also writers who are responsible for more than one book of the Bible employ different styles of writing. Yet the sum total of Scripture forms a single system of truth. This cannot be by chance. The Bible proves itself to be God's supernatural book on every level of inquiry.

Christ Is the Principal Message

Jesus Christ is the central figure of the Bible. He is the incarnate God, who came to pay the penalty for sin so that we—believers of the past, present, and future—can have a relationship with Him. From Genesis, with its symbolism of the nation that would produce the Messiah, to Revelation, where the Messiah returns in glory, the Bible presents God's love through Jesus Christ. His birth as the Jewish Messiah and Savior of the world was prophesied by Old Testament authors. Their writings contain more than three hundred separate references to the coming of Jesus, with many unique details. Bruce Wilkinson writes, "It is a unified and self-consistent portrait that centers on the person and work of Jesus Christ as its primary theme."[20]

The New Testament makes an even more revolutionary claim: Jesus Christ is the center of all biblical prophecy. "Long ago God spoke many times and in many ways to our ancestors through the prophets. And now in these final days, he has spoken to us through his Son" (Hebrews 1:1-2). The book of Ephesians declares: "God has now revealed to us his mysterious plan regarding Christ, a plan to fulfill his own good pleasure. And this is the plan: At the right time he will bring everything together under the authority of Christ—everything in heaven and on earth" (1:9-10).

The precise fulfillment of the immense body of biblical prophecy is found in one unique and revolutionary man: Jesus of Nazareth. He is the most remarkable and fascinating person in history. He has inspired more hope, taught more compassion, and shown more love than any other person who has ever lived. We can clearly see that He is the center of God's revelation to mankind.

My dear friend J.I. Packer, one of the leading biblical scholars of our time, writes,

> There is throughout [the Bible] one leading character (God the Creator), one historical perspective (world redemption),

one focal figure (Jesus of Nazareth, who is both Son of God and Savior), and one solid body of harmonious teaching about God and godliness. Truly the inner unity of the Bible is miraculous: a sign and a wonder, challenging the unbelief of our skeptical age. [21]

A Message of Love

From Genesis to Revelation, the person and work of Christ is the *main* focus of the Bible's entire theology. In turn, the central message of each book in the Bible is Christ. How could some forty different authors arrive at the same underlying theme in their works? Only through the Spirit's supernatural leading.

On Easter day 1990, I stood in the Palace of Congress inside the Kremlin walls, the most prestigious place to meet in the Soviet Union, and presented the love and forgiveness of God in Jesus Christ to six thousand Russian leaders. The authorities assured me that a potential audience of 150 million viewers was watching on television and many millions were listening by radio.

I spoke to a nation that had denied Jesus Christ and the love of God for more than seventy years. Most of the people I addressed had no knowledge of God because they had been denied Bibles for generations. As I began my message, I developed the whole of God's promise of forgiveness of sins in Christ Jesus. I was proclaiming to them the message of John 3:16: "For this is how God loved the world: He gave his one and only Son, so that everyone who believes in him will not perish but have eternal life."

Our ministry found that from 1990 to 1993, as many as 80 to 95 percent of the Russian people who attended various evangelistic events responded to the promise of John 3:16 by inviting Jesus Christ into their lives. I witnessed the same kind of response when I gave the invitation in the historic, unprecedented meeting at the Kremlin. Only God knows how many actually experienced a new birth.

Why did I focus my message to the Russian people on the person and work of Christ? Indeed, why has the love of God in Christ been my major emphasis for more than half a century of ministry? It is because the heart of the Bible's message is Christ. Jesus Himself emphasized that He was the heart of God's revelation to mankind.

The Message from Jesus

Jesus's own statements show how He considered God's message to be His own mission to earth. He said to His disciples, "If you really believed Moses, you would believe me, because he wrote about me" (John 5:46). Another time, He described how religious Jews had missed the message in times past: "You foolish people! You find it so hard to believe all that the prophets wrote in the Scriptures. Wasn't it clearly predicted that the Messiah would have to suffer all these things before entering his glory?" (Luke 24:25-26).

We learned in an earlier chapter that God often calls Himself Jehovah or I AM. Jesus claimed to be the I AM of the Old Testament. Here are some examples:

- "*I am* the bread of life" (John 6:35).
- "*I am* the light of the world" (John 8:12).
- "*I am* the gate" (John 10:9).
- "*I am* the Son of God" (John 10:36).
- "*I am* the resurrection and the life" (John 11:25).

Other names and titles of Christ found throughout Scripture show how important He is to God's plan for the universe. Jesus is called the cornerstone (Psalm 118:22), the arm of the Lord (Isaiah 51:9 NIV), the Anointed One (Daniel 9:25), the messenger of the covenant (Malachi 3:1), Son of the Most High (Luke 1:32), the Lamb of God (John 1:29), Mediator (1 Timothy 2:5), Root of David (Revelation 5:5 NIV), and the Word of God (Revelation 19:13). Clearly, these texts show that Jesus is the centerpiece of history.

The Message of the New Testament Writers

My mother became a Christian at the age of sixteen during an old-fashioned Methodist revival meeting. Later she became a schoolteacher. Still later as a mother she spent endless hours reading her Bible and praying for her family long before the break of day and long after dark. The New Testament was especially meaningful to her. She was ninety-three when she went to be with our Lord.

You can imagine that after so many years, the Bibles she read were well tattered from much use. And you can be sure that her Bible was stained with tears as she daily brought to the Lord her petitions on behalf of her family, loved ones, and others.

My heart beats with affection and deep gratitude to God when I think of my saintly mother and the rich heritage she left for me, our family, and many others who were exposed to her godly life. To her, the New Testament was the most meaningful literature of her long and fruitful life.

Like her, I am amazed at how perfectly God put together the New Testament. It grew book by book, from decade to decade. As the Holy Spirit inspired special men of God, they witnessed to Christ's life, death, and resurrection. They recorded the miracles they had seen and the love they had experienced through their exposure to God's beloved Son. He is the leading figure in all four Gospel accounts, the one who sends His Spirit on the Day of Pentecost, who retains all rights to build His church throughout the book of Acts, the ground of justification and the standard for holy living in all the Epistles, and the King of kings and Lord of lords in the book of Revelation.

From the beginning of the New Testament to the end, the writers are in complete harmony. For example, in Matthew 1:1 Jesus Christ is called a "descendant of King David." In Revelation 22:16 He is called the "source of David." The unity is complete.

Christ in the Old Testament

The Old Testament also places Jesus Christ as the center of history, but He is named as the Messiah and King of the Jews rather than as

Jesus. In the Old Testament, the work of Christ was not fully revealed as it is in the New Testament, yet the seed is there. This seed is shown through types and shadows, which are references to Jesus in a more symbolic way. Sometimes the death and resurrection of Jesus is shown through an Old Testament story, such as Noah's ark (like Noah, Jesus is our "ark" who preserves us from eternal destruction). Christ's atoning sacrifice is foreshadowed in the Israelite worship rituals performed in the Tabernacle (the blood sacrifices made by the priests in the temple show the type of death Jesus would die to save humankind).

The following chart shows a few of the types and shadows with both Old and New Testament references. Look up some of them to see how the New Testament is true to the Old Testament picture of Christ.

TYPE OR SHADOW		
	OT Reference	NT Reference
Jesus as the Lamb	Isaiah 53:7	John 1:29
Jesus as High Priest	Genesis 14:18	Hebrews 5:5-6
Jesus as a sacrificial ram	Genesis 22:9-14	Hebrews 10:5-10
Jesus in the Passover	Exodus 12:1-13	1 Peter 1:18-19
Jesus as the bread of life	Exodus 16:35	John 6:49-51
Jesus as the rock	Exodus 17:6	1 Corinthians 10:1-4
Jesus in the experiences of Jonah	Jonah 1:17	Matthew 12:39-40

It has been said, "Touch the Bible anywhere, and you touch Christ somewhere." Only by divine revelation and inspiration could those who preached and taught hundreds of years before Christ walked the earth depict His person and work with such astounding accuracy.

When I think of how much the Bible honors and exalts Christ, I am reminded of the poignant words of Saint Patrick, who said, "Christ be with me, Christ within me, Christ behind me, Christ before me, Christ beside me, Christ to win me, Christ to comfort and restore me, Christ beneath me, Christ above me, Christ in quiet, Christ in danger, Christ in hearts of all that love me, Christ in mouth of friend and stranger."[22] Dear friends, this is my prayer for you as well as for myself—that you too will be full of Christ. But this will not happen unless you are first full of His Word.

Following the Bible

Being full of Christ's Word means using it to guide your life. Before the advent of electronic navigation, a certain harbor in Italy could be reached only by sailing up a narrow channel between hazardous rocks and shoals. Many ship captains who were either unfamiliar with the harbor's design or simply disregarded the threat it posed caused their ships to be wrecked there. To help guide ships safely into port, three lights were mounted on three huge poles in the harbor. When the three lights were perfectly lined up and seen as one, a ship could safely turn to begin navigation up the narrow channel. If the pilot saw two or three lights separately, he knew that he was off course and in danger. He must continue to maneuver his vessel until the lights perfectly lined up.

The same rules of navigation that apply to the harbor pilot also apply to readers of the Bible. Because all Scripture has God as its author, all of its parts line up perfectly. This is what we call the *organic unity* of the Bible. Therefore, navigating the Scriptures safely requires us to keep each book, each author, and each doctrine of Scripture where God placed them—in perfect agreement. The Bible's incredible unity is one of the clearest proofs of its supernatural origin.

To assist you in understanding the unity of the Bible and its components and to give you a better handle on how to navigate through the Bible, the Discover the Treasure study will show you the main sections of the Bible. Work through the questions so that you can fully benefit from the exciting material about God's promises given in the next chapter.

Then consult appendix A, "Summaries of the Books of the Bible," for a wonderful overview of the Bible. Note the summaries of the biblical books as well as short introductions to each of the Bible's major divisions. Read through the summaries and introductions to see the grand sweep of the Bible's message; then use the appendix as a resource throughout your Bible study.

DISCOVER THE TREASURE

To become familiar with your own Bible, leaf through it and look at the divisions outlined below. If possible, use a Bible with headings to help you answer the questions.

The Bible is composed of two main sections: the Old Testament and the New Testament. The Old Testament records events before the time of Christ; the New Testament begins with the life of Jesus and covers the birth of the early church. The Old Testament contains thirty-nine books; the New Testament twenty-seven books.

Read Genesis 1 and Revelation 22.

From these two chapters, briefly summarize the scope of the contents of the Bible.

The Old Testament

The Old Testament can be divided into five parts. These parts are not chronological but are arranged according to the type of book. List the books in each section.

Pentateuch: Most theologians believe that Moses wrote the first five books of law and history.

1.

2.

3.

4.

5.

Historical books: The next twelve books tell of the establishment of the kingdom of Israel, of the nation's repeated turning from God to sin, and Israel's exile.

Kingdom era books:

    1.

    2.

    3.

Duration of the kingdom books:

    4.

    5.

    6.

    7.

    8.

    9.

Exile books:

    10.

    11.

    12.

Poetry: Of the next five books, Psalms—the Hebrew hymnbook—is probably the best known.

    1.

    2.

3.

4.

5.

Major Prophets: Written shortly before Israel was taken into captivity during the exile, these five books prophesy the coming Messiah and other world events.

1.

2.

3.

4.

5.

Minor Prophets: These last twelve books of the Old Testament are called minor only because they are shorter. They mainly concern Israel and the coming Messiah.

1.

2.

3.

4.

5.

6.

7.

8.

9.

10.

11.

12.

The New Testament

The New Testament can also be divided into five parts.

Gospels: The first four books tell of Christ's life and ministry.

1.

2.

3.

4.

Acts: This history of the early church describes the ministries of Paul and Peter. How does the book start (1:1-3) and how does it end (28:29-31)?

Pauline Epistles and Hebrews: Thirteen of the letters were written by Paul and were named for the church or individual to whom they were sent. Although the author of Hebrews is not identified, some believe Paul also wrote that book.

1.

2.

3.

4.

5.

6.

7.

8.

9.

10.

11.

12.

13.

14.

General Epistles: These seven letters are named not for their recipients but for their writers.

1.

2.

3.

4.

5.

6.

7.

Revelation: The last book of the New Testament is one of prophecy. It describes the end times and the triumph of Christ in His second coming. Describe the central message of Revelation (22:12-17).

4

What Does the Bible Promise?

Let me take you back thousands of years to the time of Abraham. He had a unique relationship with God, one that was deep and personal. Because of Abraham's faith, God planned to use him to bless the entire world. This blessing would be given through Abraham's descendants, which would include the Son of David, Jesus Christ. This is what God said to Abraham:

> Then the LORD said to him, "No, your servant will not be your heir, for you will have a son of your own who will be your heir." Then the LORD took Abram outside and said to him, "Look up into the sky and count the stars if you can. That's how many descendants you will have!"
>
> And Abram believed the LORD, and the LORD counted him as righteous because of his faith (Genesis 15:5-6).

But the promise to Abraham came with testing. First, Abraham and his wife, Sarah, had no children. How could Abraham have thousands of descendants if he had no children? But God provided a miracle. When Abraham and Sarah were very old—well beyond childbearing years—Sarah gave birth to a son.

Then one day God asked something of Abraham that was unthinkable—to sacrifice that son, Isaac, on an altar as an act of worship to Him. But what of the promise? How would the blessings come to the nations if Isaac was dead?

It's not hard to imagine what Abraham must have felt as he and Isaac made the trek to the place God designated. The drama came to a head on Mount Moriah as Abraham laid his son on the altar and stretched out a knife to slay him. But no matter how badly things looked at the moment, Abraham was confident that God would not betray His promise.

Suddenly, a voice from heaven said, "Abraham! Abraham!"

"Yes," Abraham said. "Here I am!"

The voice was God's, and He said, "Don't lay a hand on the boy! Do not hurt him in any way, for now I know that you truly fear God. You have not withheld from me even your son, your only son" (Genesis 22:11-12).

Abraham lifted his eyes and saw a ram caught in the thicket. In the ram, we can see not only Isaac's salvation but also one of the clearest pictures in the Old Testament of Christ—our substitute at the Cross. John the Baptist declared of Jesus, "Look! The Lamb of God who takes away the sin of the world!" (John 1:29). While the picture of Christ as the Lamb of God is keenly portrayed in the ram that Abraham saw in the thicket, we also see in the person of Abraham the picture of our heavenly Father's willingness to sacrifice His only Son. Through God's promise and Abraham's obedient faith, we can better grasp the New Testament concept of how our heavenly Father loves the world so much that He willingly sacrificed His only Son (John 3:16).

God promised to bless all the nations of the earth through Abraham's descendants. This blessing foreshadows the universal blessing of the gospel of Christ. Paul writes, "And now that you belong to Christ, you are the true children of Abraham. You are his heirs, and God's promise to Abraham belongs to you" (Galatians 3:29).

God's Promises Prove His Love

The promises in God's Word are the proof of His love for us. They mean so much to me that I wrote a book of daily devotions called *Promises: A Daily Guide to Supernatural Living*, which includes 365 of the promises in God's Word.

I have tested God's promises throughout my lifetime and have found them to be sure. As relatively new Christians in 1951, Vonette and I surrendered our lives totally and completely to the Lord Jesus to do with as He wished. We didn't do it for any personal honor, glory, praise, or material benefit; we did it because we loved Him and we wanted to obey His command as recorded in Mark 8:34: "Whoever wants to be my disciple must deny themselves and take up their cross and follow me" (NIV).

After we had made this commitment, we discovered that God promises abundant benefits and blessings to all who will truly follow Him. As the years passed, I looked back to consider the promise that God will reward us for whatever we give up for His sake. Have I received more money than I gave up? Have I received more in other ways than we sacrificed that Sunday afternoon in 1951?

As I meditate on what Mark 8:34 means, I become excited over what God has done, and is still doing, in my life and Vonette's. For example, it is conceivable that had I continued in business, which was very profitable, I could have made millions of dollars to give to the cause of Christ. Suppose I had given a million in a lifetime—or a million a year. It would not compare with the many millions of dollars that have been released to Christ and His kingdom through the ministry of Campus Crusade for Christ. Through this experience, I learned that God's promises are immeasurable.

A "Check" in God's Bank

We can think of God's promises as promissory notes written to us. A promissory note is a written assurance, like a contract, to pay on demand or at a certain time a fixed amount of money to a specific person or group. God has written us a "check" that we can bring to His spiritual "bank" to cash.

God's promises fall into two categories—unconditional and conditional. An unconditional promise is one that God offers and guarantees without any "ifs" included. An example of an unconditional promise would be the one God made to Noah after the Great Flood that destroyed almost all of mankind. After Noah came out of the ark, God said,

"Yes, I am confirming my covenant with you. Never again will floodwaters kill all living creatures; never again will a flood destroy the earth."

Then God said, "I am giving you a sign of my covenant with you and with all living creatures, for all generations to come. I have placed my rainbow in the clouds. It is the sign of my covenant with you and with all the earth" (Genesis 9:11-13).

Noah didn't have to do anything to receive the promise, and he didn't have to maintain any standards to continue the promise. God gave the promise with no strings attached.

God gives other promises that are conditional, that require the recipients to do something to obtain the blessing. Here is a promise from Matthew 6:33: "Seek the Kingdom of God above all else, and live righteously, and he will give you everything you need." The promise is that we will receive an abundance of blessings from God, but the benefit will not be fulfilled until we put Him first in our lives. That is the condition that makes the promise possible.

The Bible contains one specific kind of promise called a *covenant*. God's covenants are binding contracts He establishes between Himself and a person or group of people. God's covenants include promises that He will never break.

The promise that God gave to Abraham is a covenant. So was the promise given to Noah. The most vital covenant to us is the New Covenant. As Jesus passed the cup of wine to His disciples at the Last Supper, He promised, "Each of you drink from it, for this is my blood, which confirms the covenant between God and His people. It is poured out as a sacrifice to forgive the sins of many" (Matthew 26:27-28). This is the most precious promise in the Bible: We can have forgiveness of sin through Christ's sacrifice on the cross. From it flows all the other promises God has given to Christians.

Just think of all the things God has promised you in the Scriptures. He has chosen not to leave you ignorant of how you can obtain the blessings of eternal life. He shines His light into your heart so that you might know how to experience a fruitful and abundant life of service in His kingdom.

The Beauty of God's Promises

The Scottish pastor and writer Thomas Guthrie could not find enough metaphors to describe the inexhaustible blessings a Christian enjoys by following the teachings of the Bible. He said, "The Bible is an armory of heavenly weapons, a laboratory of infallible medicines, a mine of exhaustless wealth. It is a guidebook for every road, a chart for every sea, a medicine for every malady, and a balm for every wound. Rob us of our Bible and our sky has lost its sun."[23]

Guthrie expressed what I feel about the Bible and the promises it contains. Who can imagine all the wonders that God has in store for us? And these assurances are plainly written for us to understand.

If you have read a contract recently, you know how complicated people make legal transactions. A house mortgage has so many pages that it forms a good-size book. The language the mortgage contains is almost indecipherable unless you have some training in how to read it.

On the other hand, God's promises are simple and clear. They are warm and personal. If they have conditions, the conditions are doable. If they have consequences, the results are well defined. Let me give you a few examples:

Simple and clear: "You can pray for anything, and if you have faith, you will receive it" (Matthew 21:22).

Warm and personal: "Those who fear the LORD are secure; he will be a refuge for their children" (Proverbs 14:26).

Doable: "Don't worry about anything; instead, pray about everything. Tell God what you need, and thank him for all he has done. Then you will experience God's peace, which exceeds anything we can understand. His peace will guard your hearts and minds as you live in Christ Jesus" (Philippians 4:6-7).

Clear consequences: "Don't be misled—you cannot mock the justice of God. You will always harvest what you plant" (Galatians 6:7).

The promises of God are sure. Just as a promissory note is backed up by the person who issued it, God's promises are backed up by His character and riches. How sure are His promises? God tells us that He will not change His mind about what He has said (Numbers 23:19). The New Testament explains how firm God's Word is:

> Now when people take an oath, they call on someone greater than themselves to hold them to it. And without any question that oath is binding. God also bound himself with an oath, so that those who received the promise could be perfectly sure that he would never change his mind. So God has given both his promise and his oath. These two things are unchangeable because it is impossible for God to lie. Therefore, we who have fled to him for refuge can have great confidence as we hold to the hope that lies before us (Hebrews 6:16-18).

Do these verses give you as much faith in God's Word as they do me? We could not depend on anyone greater than God—and He will fulfill all He says. We can count on God to live up to what He promises.

God also will never give up on what He says. "Understand, therefore, that the LORD your God is indeed God. He is the faithful God who keeps his covenant for a thousand generations and lavishes his unfailing love on those who love him and obey his commands" (Deuteronomy 7:9). In the New Testament, Hebrews 10:23 assures us, "Let us hold tightly without wavering to the hope we affirm, for God can be trusted to keep his promise."

We have all had the miserable experience of having a friend betray us by going back on his promise. That kind of failure can cause a friendship to break or to suffer serious disruption. But that will never happen with God. He will never betray any of His promises.

God's Promises in Hard Times

We must never underestimate the power of God's promises. Since 1994, Campus Crusade for Christ has sponsored a Fasting and Prayer Conference each year. During Fasting and Prayer '99, a prayer request for a woman who was about to appear in bankruptcy court was brought to the attention of several attendees. She was a single mom with four children, one of whom was diabetic, and the woman was about to lose her home. While she was in court, caring people gathered to pray that God would move the judge's heart to show mercy. They relied on the promise that God will work out things for our good according to His will (Romans 8:28). We later learned that the judge, against all precedent, not only allowed the woman to keep her home but also gave her five years to repay her debt. Truly God moves when His people pray.

Whenever hard times come, we can go to God's Word for help—no matter how badly things look. Years ago the wife of André Kole, the talented illusionist who has been on the staff of Campus Crusade for Christ for many years, had an incurable brain tumor, and for two years Aljeana endured incredible suffering. She gradually lost the use of her arms and legs and could not move her head or body. She became totally blind. Day after day she could do nothing but lie helplessly in bed. André and Aljeana were my dear friends and colleagues, and my heart was broken for them.

While Aljeana was still able to do some speaking, she always shared a poem that ended with these lines: "We should not long for heaven, if earth held only joy." One day as I visited her in the hospital, I observed her usual radiant smile. "Why are you smiling?" I asked.

"Oh, God is so good to me. I am rejoicing in His presence."

Aljeana was a woman who followed Jesus with her whole heart, mind, soul, and strength until the day she saw Him face-to-face. She knew His promises to be real, and she held tightly to the truth of her eternal inheritance until the end. Peace, joy, and blessing are promised us in our daily walk with Christ, and at the same time we can anticipate a glorious home in heaven, which Christ's death purchased for those who love Him.

Promises for Daily Living

Many of the promises, particularly in the New Testament and in Psalms and Proverbs, help us to live godly lives. One of the promises that I have claimed many times over the years is that God will help us resist temptation.

As a new Christian, I was faced with a temptation that was

threatening to destroy my Christian walk and witness. In the process I memorized 1 Corinthians 10:13: "The temptations in your life are no different from what others experience. And God is faithful. He will not allow the temptation to be more than you can stand. When you are tempted, he will show you a way out so that you can endure." God dramatically fulfilled that promise for me then as He has on similar occasions through the years.

I have learned that whenever a temptation comes, I can claim this promise. No matter what the nature of it, God faithfully deals with the temptation. I simply remember 1 Corinthians 10:13 and say to the Lord Jesus, "I can't handle this temptation. I surrender to You." Then I thank Him for taking care of it—for carrying the load for me. He has always been faithful to His promise.

You will be able to find many other promises that will help you become more like Christ. The secret is in studying and reading the Bible daily. As we dig deeper into the treasure of God's Word, we will find more promises. In fact, the word *promise* (and its variations) is used hundreds of times in the Bible. And many other passages assure us of God's promises without directly using that word.

Of course, before we claim one of God's promises, we make sure that promise was meant for us. God has given many promises to His people, the nation of Israel. We must not claim these promises for our lives in inappropriate ways. Instead, look at the verses around the passage with the promise to see to whom the verses were written. Also, check with other portions of Scripture to make sure that your interpretation of the passage is correct.

Praying Through Scripture

One way many people incorporate God's promises into their lives is by praying through Scripture. Jane McClain writes, "In the Book of Isaiah God promises that His Word 'will not return to me empty, but will accomplish what I desire' (55:11). I find that whenever I pray Scripture—whether I'm praying it word for word or using it as a springboard for prayer—I experience the truth of this miraculous promise. I am enriched in the process of returning God's Word to him to be fulfilled."[24]

We can use God's promises to receive His blessing; it's like cashing in a spiritual promissory note. We can also use God's promises to praise Him for all He is doing for us. Scriptures can guide our prayers to help us fulfill God's requirements for our lives. The Discover the Treasure material at the end of this chapter will show you how to begin praying through Scripture.

Part 2—"How Can I Understand the Bible?"—will show you how to dig into God's Word on your own. You will find that these simple Bible study methods are exciting and easy to use. When you learn to discover biblical principles on your own, you can begin making the Bible the foundation for your life. It truly will be the greatest treasure hunt you will ever undertake.

DISCOVER THE TREASURE

Our prayers should include four elements. To help you remember these elements, remember the word *ACTS.*

1. **Adoration:** Praise God for who He is.

2. **Confession:** Admit your sin to God.

3. **Thanksgiving:** Thank God for His character and blessings.

4. **Supplication:** Tell God your concerns and requests.

You can incorporate all of these in your plan for praying through Scripture. Select a passage that is meaningful to you or goes along with the topic in your devotions for the day.

Follow these steps:

1. Read the passage.

2. Write your answer to these questions: What promise or command is in this passage? What lesson do I need to learn?

3. Write down what you want to say to God as a result of what you discovered. Make sure that you have

something for each prayer action (**A**doration, **C**onfession, **T**hanksgiving, and **S**upplication). Your responses can be either Scripture that you say back to God or expressions of your own heart.

4. Pray what you've written.

Example: If you selected Romans 8:26-30, you might answer the questions this way:

What promise is in these verses? The Holy Spirit will help me pray.

What command must I obey? I must love God.

What lesson do I need to learn? God causes everything in my life to work out for my good.

Your prayer: *God, You are so wonderful. You are so involved in my life that You see my prayers and help me pray when my heart is heavy. I am sorry that I haven't taken more time to talk to You in the past twenty-four hours. I thank You that You are patient with me and will still work in my life for my good even though I fail You at times. Please help me to bring all my problems and joys to You. In Jesus's name, amen.*

The following list provides some suggestions for passages you can use to begin.

- Psalm 91:9-13
- Psalm 141:1-4
- Proverbs 2:1-5
- Matthew 6:25-27
- Galatians 5:16-18
- Philippians 4:8-9

PART 2

How Can I Understand the Bible?

"The Bible is the greatest work of literature, history, and theology ever written. In its production, preservation, proclamation, and product (changed history, changed lives), it stands as the most unique book in existence."
BRUCE WILKINSON AND KENNETH BOA

5

How Can the Bible Guide My Life?

Can you imagine living alone in darkness for six months? During his first Antarctic expedition, Admiral Richard E. Byrd lived alone in a small hut that sheltered him from the brutal six-month-long winter night. He was totally isolated from the human race.

His test of endurance was quite a feat. Blasts of biting arctic wind and blowing snow buried his small hut every night. Each day Admiral Byrd shoveled his way to the surface of the snow. When he broke through, the light was so dim that he could see only a dozen yards. If he left his hut, he used the stovepipe sticking out of the snow as a reference point to find his way back.

One day when Byrd turned to go back, he couldn't see the stovepipe. Panic gripped him. His first instinct was to search for the stovepipe by walking in one direction or another. But he refused to move. He knew the danger. If he wandered about looking for his hut, he would probably get confused about where he was and would get farther and farther from the safety of his hut.

Instead, he drove a stake into the snow. Using it as a center, he paced around in a large circle looking for the entrance to his hut. He kept an eye on the stake while searching through the darkness. Not finding his hut, he extended his radius and made a bigger circle.

The third time he tried, his circle was so large that he almost lost sight of his stake. He returned and resolved to make one more attempt with an even larger circle.

As he made the fourth round, he strained to peer through the darkness. He knew if he lost sight of the stake—his reference point—he would quickly succumb to the ice and snow.

But the fourth time, he walked right into the hut's tunnel.[1]

Do you ever feel as if you are wandering through darkness in your life? Perhaps you are facing a moral question in your job and just don't know how to resolve it. Or maybe you are having a conflict with a family member, and you know your reactions are not appropriate. At times all of us feel as if we don't know what to do. Circumstances can overwhelm us. Ailing parents, an uncertain job, a high mortgage payment, mounting bills, family crises, illnesses, and other problems can make us wonder how we will ever find our way out of our quandary.

Most people use society's wisdom to figure out how to solve their problems. But that is a dangerous way to live. Cultural opinions change over time or are sometimes just wrong.

The Bible is a reference point, a true north that will guide the compass of our lives to the truth. When we stake our lives on the Bible's teachings and principles, God shows us how to live. But if we lose sight of God's wisdom, we will feel as if we are in a blinding blizzard, unable to tell which way to go.

Our Standard for Life

I have always believed that it is important for every believer to be grounded in the basic teachings of the Bible, and for many years I have worked to help disciple millions of men and women all over the world in an effort to increase their basic Bible knowledge. Let me describe several areas in which the Bible will guide your life.

The Bible tells us about God's love. Before Vonette and I married, I lived in California and she attended college in Texas. As a result, we wrote letters to each other. Each letter I got from her was a treasure. I'd read it and reread it, poring over every word. From those letters I learned more about who Vonette is and of her love for me.

The Bible is God's love letter to us. It tells us not only who He is but also the breadth of His love for us as His unique creations. To learn more about God's love for us, we must *read* His love letters, not ignore them. Can you imagine how Vonette would have felt if I had put her letters away in a drawer and ignored them, allowing several letters to stack up before I opened them and read them? Sometimes that's the way we treat God's love letter to us. We say, "The Bible isn't all that important. I'll read it later. I'm just too busy today." Ask yourself, "What is so important that it takes the place of reading my love letter from God?" As you read and reread God's love letter to you, His love will ground you in the truth, helping you see yourself and your world in a balanced perspective.

The Bible tells us about our worth. We've all heard people spout moral or political views that just don't match up with reality. The theory of evolution doesn't begin to describe the reality of how our world and its people came into existence. Somehow, some way, a blob of matter (we still don't know how the blob got there) became billions of planets, galaxies, and suns. Then in another unexplainable event, some slimy, sticky ooze turned into living matter and began to reproduce.

I can't imagine that anyone who has witnessed the birth of a child can accept the theory of evolution. Touching the tiny fingers and toes and watching the little chest rise with each breath of new life is a reminder of the life God breathed into the first person He created. The Bible tells us that we did not have a chance beginning. God made each of us as a one-of-a-kind person. He knew each of us intimately before we were even born. The psalmist expresses it so eloquently:

> You made all the delicate, inner parts of my body
>   and knit me together in my mother's womb...
> You watched me as I was being formed in utter seclusion,
>   as I was woven together in the dark of the womb.
> You saw me before I was born.
>   Every day of my life was recorded in your book.
> Every moment was laid out
>   before a single day had passed.
>   (Psalm 139:13-16)

God's Word tells us about our world and our worth.

The Bible tells us about human nature. The Bible also guides our thinking about our essential nature. Some esteemed philosophers describe humans as basically good. When asked why there is so much evil in the world, these philosophers suggest that a person's environment may influence him to do wrong or that a chemical imbalance in the brain may have caused her evil behavior. There may be some truth in these statements, but they certainly can't explain Hitler's "final solution" or a serial killer's murderous spree or the terrorist bombings of the World Trade Center. They can't explain why most two-year-olds hate to share their toys or why we have an urge to strike back when someone hurts us.

But the Bible's record of the fall of mankind in the Garden of Eden guides us in our understanding of human nature. The New Testament also reminds us that "everyone has sinned; we all fall short of God's glorious standard" (Romans 3:23). These biblical descriptions of our nature make perfect sense. They guide us in our understanding of ourselves and others.

The Bible guides the growth of our faith. The great American evangelist Dwight L. Moody was instrumental in bringing thousands of people to Christ. He once wrote:

> I prayed for faith and thought that someday faith would come down and strike me like lightning. But faith did not seem to come. One day I read in the tenth chapter of Romans, "Faith cometh by hearing, and hearing by the Word of God." I had up to this time closed my Bible and prayed for faith. I now opened my Bible and began to study, and faith has been growing ever since.[2]

God's Word guides our faith. We can attempt great things for God when our faith is grounded on the truths in His Word. We need to study the Word carefully and interpret it correctly so that we not only possess its truth, but its truth possesses us.

The Bible guides us in our witness for Christ. The greatest spiritual harvest of all time is taking place today. Thousands of people are hearing the gospel, receiving Christ as their Savior, and committing themselves to fulfill the Great Commission of our Lord to go into every part of the world and tell everyone about our Savior (Matthew 28:18-20). How is this revolution taking place? Through the distribution and teaching of God's Word by faithful Christians who want to share their joy and victory in Christ with others.

Spending time daily in God's Word gives us the power and excitement to spread His message of love and forgiveness. Studying the Bible helps us see how God loves the unlovable and seeks the lonely and hurting.

The Bible guides us when we are tempted. Every day we face temptations and situations that can harm our minds and our spirits. The Bible helps us recognize wrong thinking and bad attitudes—in ourselves and others. The New Testament describes the spiritual armor that we must carry into battle in our world. Our armor includes the "sword of the Spirit, which is the word of God" (Ephesians 6:17).

The sword was the Roman soldier's principal offensive weapon—just as the Bible must be for us. The Roman sword had a sharp edge on each side of the blade, making it a fearful weapon. That is how the apostle Paul describes the Bible: "For the word of God is alive and active. Sharper than any double-edged sword, it penetrates even to dividing soul and spirit, joints and marrow; it judges the thoughts and attitudes of the heart" (Hebrews 4:12 NIV). It would be unthinkable for a Roman soldier to go into battle without being trained in how to use his sword. The Roman soldiers trained for hours to be able to wield their weapons with the greatest effectiveness. As we study the Bible and learn its truths, we too will be able to protect ourselves. We will be able to deal with temptation.

The Word of Truth in Our Lives

I have observed two kinds of Bible readers—those who skim the surface and those who dig deep. The characteristics of the butterfly and bee help us understand the two kinds of readers.

Butterfly Readers

Butterfly readers flit around, having no patience for such dull and long-winded details. It is as if they do not consider the Bible important enough for serious consideration. Why do some people neglect the importance of the Bible? Let me suggest several reasons:

1. Some people neglect the Bible because they are not true believers. Rodney Smith was an English evangelist who made more than forty evangelistic trips abroad to such countries as the United States, Australia, and South Africa. He told of a man who said he had received no inspiration from the Bible although he had "gone through it several times." "Let it go through *you* once," replied Smith, "then you will tell a different story."

As I mentioned earlier, before I became a Christian, God's Word did not make any sense to me. I tried to read it on occasion, but I found it boring and confusing. I was a butterfly reader. Finally I concluded that no really intelligent person could believe the Bible. When I became a Christian, my life was transformed and my attitude about the Scriptures changed. I realized the Bible was truly the holy, inspired Word of God. The change happened because the Holy Spirit was living in me, and He opened my eyes to the Word. Today the Bible is my spiritual food, dearer to me than any other book in the world. I have become a bee reader.

2. Some people don't read the Bible because they are unfamiliar with biblical elements. A humorous story is told about Joseph Parker, former minister of the City Temple in London. A woman waited for Parker in his vestry after a service to thank him for the help she received from his sermons. "You do throw such wonderful light on the Bible, Doctor," she said. "Do you know that until this morning, I had always thought that Sodom and Gomorrah were man and wife?"

The Bible is full of events that took place centuries ago and stories that at first glance may appear to have no application to real-life problems. But these don't give the true essence of the Scriptures. The Bible is as contemporary as the latest newspaper or the most current magazine. It speaks to the heart of every modern issue in ways that will amaze you. Do not let the fact that the events of Scripture happened centuries ago sway you from discovering its continuing relevance. Read the Bible while prayerfully asking God to open your heart and mind to its truth, and you will quickly see how it still provides answers to every need.

3. Many people don't read the Bible because they think it will be boring. Many people treat the Bible like a library of facts rather than as a living book. When we approach Scripture as the means to know God, His precious promises, and the abundant life He offers, studying His Word becomes an adventure. George Mueller of Bristol, a pastor known for his deep faith and effective prayer life, made this statement after having read through the Bible one hundred times with increasing delight: "I look upon it as a lost day when I have not had a good time over the Word of God." Do you have a "good time" over the Word of God? You will the moment you see Scripture as the repository of all God's blessings and promises that are available to you today.

Bee Readers

I want to help you become a bee reader in your study of the Bible—a reader who knows how to dig deeply, one who is able to find the deep nectar of God's Word. Many believers call this process "rightly dividing" the Bible. The apostle Paul writes to young Timothy: "Be diligent to present yourself approved to God, a worker who does not need to be ashamed, rightly dividing the word of truth" (2 Timothy 2:15 NKJV). Other Bible versions refer to this as correctly handling or correctly explaining the Word of Truth.

Scripture is not only to be read but also studied. The great reformer Martin Luther explained his approach to dividing the Word this way:

> I study my Bible like I gather apples. First, I shake the whole tree that the ripest may fall. Then I shake each limb, and when I have shaken each limb, I shake each branch and every twig. Then I look under every leaf. I search the Bible as a whole like shaking the whole tree. Then I shake every limb—study book after book. Then I shake every branch, giving attention to the chapters. Then I shake every twig, or a careful study of the paragraphs and sentences and words and their meanings.[3]

When we study the Bible, we must peel back the layers of such things as the author's intent, historical context, and use of grammar to reach the depths of God's Word and its meaning for our lives. And we must employ our skills with utmost reverence for the Word.

Where do we begin to learn how to accurately handle the Bible? Effective Bible interpretation begins with a commitment to both reading and studying the Bible consistently. An old truism states: "A Bible in the hand is worth two in the bookcase." We do not become proficient in Bible study unless we are willing to take our Bible off the shelf and spend time with it. Just as our physical bodies require wholesome food daily for good health, so our spiritual beings require God's Word daily for spiritual health and growth. The more time we spend in Scripture, the more it will transform our lives and the more we will be able to gain true knowledge and discernment.

Digging Deeper

Getting to know the Bible involves having a well-rounded plan for digging into God's message. To keep moving along the path of righteousness and walking with God in a fast-track world, we need to set aside time with Him, reading, memorizing, and studying His Word.

Build a plan for these activities into your schedule. Be flexible. Listen for the Holy Spirit's prompting about your pace and method. Do not become discouraged if you fail to make your appointment with God one day. Good habits take work to develop. Ask God to give you the motivation to stay on course.

Just as a motor runs smoothly when all its parts are balanced, our spiritual lives need to have balance too. Let me offer a few guidelines on how to prioritize your Bible reading and study time.

1. Set aside fifteen minutes every day for a quiet time. The purpose of a quiet time is to enjoy the Lord and communicate with Him about every detail of your day. As you read a portion of Scripture and pray each day, you allow Him to speak to you in a personal way.

Some people like to read through a small portion of Scripture and meditate on it. Others like to use daily devotional books, which usually have a short Bible passage and a brief reading to go along with the passage. Your local Christian bookstore contains a wide variety of devotional books.

Use a notebook to record insights from God's Word, your prayer requests, praises to God, and thanks for answered prayer. For the last few minutes of your quiet time, just listen to God. Ask Him to speak to you through His Word. Think about what you have read, and thank Him for all He has done for you.

2. *Allow fifteen minutes each day to read through the Bible in a year.* I recommend reading the Bible from cover to cover. For many years, I have read the entire Bible during a twelve-month period. This has been one of the richest blessings in my life. John Stott, a great British missionary statesman, recommended reading three chapters each day and studying one in depth. With this plan, you will complete the Bible in a year. But take into account that some chapters are much longer than others, so the time you spend each day will vary. (The Discover the Treasure section at the end of this chapter will give suggestions for how you can read the Bible in a year.)

3. *Take a few minutes each day to memorize Scripture.* Have you started memorizing Scripture? We discussed its importance in chapter 2. How have the verses you learned challenged or helped you in your daily life? I encourage you to keep working at it. Memorization will become much easier as you do it consistently.

4. *Dedicate a few hours each week to Bible study.* As I mentioned earlier, Bible reading and Bible study are two different activities. Study is time dedicated to digging deeper. Plan a specific time and place to work on these studies. Vonette and I begin every day in prayer together, usually just for five minutes. Then we separate and study the Word of God individually.

If you are a Bible-study newcomer, begin with about half an hour a week and add more time as you go. Decide where you will study, perhaps in a quiet corner in your home that you can designate for Bible study. You may find it more productive to work at a desk or table. If you already use the computer for other tasks, you may prefer to keep your files and notes on it. Sometimes you will want to study the Bible on your own, working through a particular book of the Bible or examining the life of a Bible character. Other times, God may lead you to study with a friend or to join a small-group study.

Before you begin, you may want to obtain a few study aids. Many Bible students have found these tools to be very helpful:

- *Study Bible:* Start with a comprehensive study Bible that will give notes about various verses, overviews of books of the Bible, time lines, outlines, maps, cross-references to related Scripture verses, an index, and a dictionary/concordance.

- *Concordance:* A Bible concordance is an alphabetical index of key words and where they are found in the Bible.

- *Bible dictionary:* A Bible dictionary gives descriptions of names, places, things, and events found in the Bible.

- *Study guide:* Bible-study guides give questions and insights that help readers unpack the meaning of a Bible book or passage. Christian bookstores offer dozens of Bible-study guides about biblical topics, characters, themes, and individual books of the Bible.

- *Bible software:* Bible software gives you the ability to search for key words and phrases, providing an instantaneous list of all the verses that contain those words. For example, an electronic search will locate all uses of the word *mercy,* as well as the immediate context where that word appears. Some software will include Bible dictionaries, encyclopedias, and even commentaries.

A word of caution: As you use your Bible-study aids, remember that Bible study involves just that—studying the *Bible.* Do not allow yourself to rely so heavily on Bible-study aids that God cannot teach you from His Word.

How you balance these four areas of relating to God's Word will depend on your situation and your spiritual needs at the moment. Some days you might have to make small adjustments in your daily routine to saturate yourself in God's Word. Other times your heart may ache, and you will want to lengthen your time to search the Scripture and to soothe your spirit with God's message of love to you.

DISCOVER THE TREASURE

I want to encourage you even more about reading through the Bible in a year. You can do that using one of two methods:

First, you can use the *The Daily Bible* from Harvest House Publishers, which divides the Bible into 365 daily readings arranged in chronological order (www.harvesthousepublishers.com). Also, Tyndale House Publishers has a number of *One Year Bible* products with daily readings from the Old Testament, New Testament, Psalms, and Proverbs (www.tyndale.com).

Second, you can use any of a number of Bible reading plans that are available on the Internet. Just do an online search for "Bible reading plans" to explore your options.

I promise you that if you commit yourself to reading through the entire Bible, you will find abundant blessing in the process. Try to keep up with the schedule every day, but if you miss a day or two here and there, don't give up. Just move on to the current day's passages and keep going.

6

How Can I Unlock the Bible's Meaning?

A few days after Dave returned to the University of Michigan for his second year of graduate school, he got an email message from a former roommate.

> dave, i know this will shock you, but i won't be coming back to school this year. the story is too long to tell right now, so i'll write a longer email later. i'm in afghanistan working as an agriculturalist in a village about two hours south of mazar-e-sharif, the headquarters of the northern alliance. i love my work. i think it's what i was created to do.
>
> and i've met someone. more about that later.
>
> look, i have a feeling i may not be back in the states for quite a while. when i left campus last year, i put three trunks in storage at baker hall. consider them yours. you'll find some good things inside—books, music, electronics, and other things. enjoy them. i may not ever want them back. i'm getting into sleeping on the floor, cooking over an open fire, living close to the land.
>
> anyway, buddy, i hope you have a good year. gotta run. i'll catch you later.
>
> ben

Dave was surprised—and saddened—by the message. He had been looking forward to seeing Ben on campus. After Dave adjusted to his friend's change of plans, he started to think about what might be in the trunks Ben left for him. Ben had an awesome library. Dave had drooled over it many times. Could those books be in the trunks? And what about Ben's CD collection? Ben may have taken a few dozen with him to Afghanistan, but the rest—hundreds of them—might be in the trunks. He grabbed his backpack and started out for Baker Hall. Then it hit him.

He had no keys to the trunks.

Unless Dave somehow gets Ben's keys, he'll never be able to unpack the trunks and enjoy the good things Ben left him. The same is true for unpacking the good things God has left for us in His Word. Unless we have the keys to unlocking the Bible's meaning, we will not be able to enjoy the life-giving message He has for us.

I would like to hand over to you several keys that will help you dig into the Bible and unlock its meaning.

Key 1: Observe Carefully

Study of the Bible begins with careful observation. It is the exercise of asking, "What do I see?" In *Living by the Book*, Dr. Howard Hendricks and William D. Hendricks remark, "What makes one person a better Bible student than another? He can see more, that's all. The same truth is available to both of them in the text. The only difference between them is what either one can see in a cubic foot of space."[4]

The psalmist understood the need for the powers of observation and prayed, "Open my eyes to see the wonderful truths in your instructions" (Psalm 119:18). God honors that prayer and sends His Holy Spirit to sharpen our sight.

There is a vital connection between careful observation and effective learning. To be better observers, we must understand two principles that make observation a valuable tool:

1. Observation is more than seeing. Think over this question: How many traffic lights do you pass on your way to work? Do you know? You see them every day on your drive to work, but you may not be observing them. Here's another question: What color was your boss's shirt at work yesterday? Difficult question? We see things all around us, yet seldom do we pay special attention. But observation requires a level of concentration and reflection. Observing things provides a much better chance of remembering them. Our Bible study must bring us past the surface vision to the deeper level of principles and eternal truths. We must go beyond facts to the heart of the message.

2. Observation is more than a set of skills. Bible study assumes an eagerness to learn. We should come to the Bible with a mind-set of openness, wonder, and even awe. Remember, this is God's holy, inspired, inerrant word of love for and to us. Your heart should be ignited with excitement to get to know more about God and what He says and thinks. Bible study is your opportunity to plumb the depths of His inspired Word, where the hidden treasures of true wisdom and understanding lie.

Key 2: Ask Questions

Closely related to observation is the need to bring curiosity to our study. Go to the Bible with your questions. This is the best way to learn. Unless we can relate to a passage of Scripture, we usually do not remember it or take anything from it. Questions provide a lively context for Bible study. Personalize your search of the Scriptures with your own questions about God, yourself, and life in general. You will be amazed at how much more meaningful your discoveries will become.

Certain general questions can work in almost any passage of Scripture. Be sure to have a pen or pencil and some paper ready to record your answers. Here are examples of typical questions a Bible student should ask:

- What does this passage say about God's character?
- What does this passage teach about Jesus Christ?
- What does this passage teach about the Holy Spirit?
- What does this passage say about how I should live?
- How does this passage direct my faith?

- What command should I obey?
- What promise should I claim for my life?
- What truth should I take seriously?
- What is the purpose of the text?

The last question—What is the purpose of the text?—is *the* most important question for ascertaining the meaning of a passage. Through this question you are attempting to discover the message the author meant to convey. I cannot tell you how many Bible studies and sermons I have heard that failed to express what the writer of Scripture wished to express. A reading of Scripture can trigger many ideas in one's mind. But your idea, although it may be a great one, may not be the writer's idea. Without a firm grasp of the writer's aim, it is impossible to understand the meaning of the passage.

For example, Luke 19 records the story of Zacchaeus. What is the purpose of this text? Does Luke want to prove that Jesus can save short tax collectors? Or is it that we should practice Christian hospitality in our homes? Although these are good points, Luke's real intent is to teach that *true* repentance results in changed behavior. Zacchaeus demonstrated this truth in his heartfelt desire to practice restitution (Luke 19:8).

Key 3: Compare Passages of Scripture

While the church has been truly blessed by many fine Bible commentaries, Bible dictionaries, and other study tools designed to unlock the meaning of the Scriptures, the best interpreter of the Bible is the Bible itself. Indeed, the Bible is the world's finest Bible commentary. Another way to express this is to say that the Bible is *self-interpreting*. We understand Bible passages in their relationship to other Bible passages.

This goes back to the unity of the Bible—that the many truths of God's Word are interdependent and interrelated. The Bible is not sixty-six books but one unfolding book of divine truth. A given text must therefore be illumined by other Scripture passages that shed light on its meaning. If one Bible passage looks as if it might mean one thing, but when compared to corollary passages appears to mean something different, you must follow the later interpretation—the one grounded in the *whole* of the Bible's teaching. The correct interpretation of a Scripture passage will always agree with the rest of the Bible. God never contradicts Himself.

For example, in Matthew 4 we read the account of Satan's attempt to get Jesus to obey him. Satan asks Jesus to leap from the pinnacle of the Temple with the Scripture's promise that angels will catch Him:

> "If you are the Son of God, jump off! For the Scriptures say,
>
> 'He will order his angels to protect you.
> And they will hold you up with their hands
> so you won't even hurt your foot on a stone.'"
> (Matthew 4:6)

Reading these words makes sense. God would never allow Jesus to be involved in anything contrary to His eternal plan. So, if we just rely on this one verse, we might conclude that Satan is correct.

But Jesus recognized that Satan was taking God's Word out of context: "Jesus responded, 'The Scriptures also say, "You must not test the LORD your God"'" (Matthew 4:7). Jesus's masterful use of the Scriptures thwarted Satan's plot. Jesus saw the complete picture—the part that Satan was covering up. The Son of God overcame Satan's tricks by knowing the whole of the Scriptures.

Key 4: Understand the Context

No one likes his or her words to be taken out of context. Many years ago, a noted religious magazine made a habit of ridiculing well-known Christian leaders. Billy Graham and Robert Schuller were favorite targets of this publication. One day I received a request to be interviewed by this magazine. I said, "No, I don't have time for people like that." Several years later, one of the outstanding leaders on our staff convinced me to take the interview with the promise from the magazine that it would print only what I said. Because I greatly respect this staff person, I agreed to the interview.

Within a few weeks not one but three people arrived to interview me. One sat on either side of me and one in front of me, and they attacked me as if they were accusing me of a crime. In their questions, they took some statements I had made and twisted them out of context and then demanded an explanation. They tried to make it a terrible experience for me. They accused me of being dishonest. They called me a liar and a hypocrite. Trying to make me angry, they said, "We'll print only what you say." They assumed that if they could get me to explode, they could print my exact words and besmirch my name.

I made one statement that they jumped on before listening to my explanation. I said, "I do not have any problems." I have said this many times, and I have a specific meaning behind the words. Without listening to my explanation, they turned my statement into an accusation, "Everyone has problems. You're a liar."

I responded to their allegation in a quiet, calm way, "Of course everybody has problems, but according to God's Word, as true believers we are supposed to cast our cares on the Lord and our cares become His concern, not ours. After all, I'm a child of God, and my Father takes care of His children."

True to their word, the editors printed only what I said. But on the cover of the next issue of the magazine, they superimposed my face on Mount Rushmore, placing mine between the faces of Thomas Jefferson and Teddy Roosevelt. Talk about being taken out of context. But I prayed for those men and believe that God used that experience in their lives as He did in mine.

We must be careful never to take the Bible's words out of context. Always interpret Scripture texts in their context, looking at the passages before the text and after it.

We must also be careful not to superimpose our own interpretation on the passage. The apostle Peter writes, "But know this first of all, that no prophecy of Scripture is a matter of one's own interpretation, for no prophecy was ever made by an act of human will, but men moved by the Holy Spirit spoke from God" (2 Peter 1:20-21 NASB). We should not manipulate the Bible's text to fit our personal interpretation. As we just learned from Satan's *mis*use of Scripture, we can get the Bible to say just about anything.

Understanding verses and passages in their context is an important step in making sure we are not manipulating the Bible. Bible scholar J.I. Packer observes:

> We do not want to make the terrible mistake of "reading in" to the Bible our own private interpretation. We cannot arrive at a true understanding of God's Word by detaching texts from their contexts to find personal meaning in them and by feeding them into the world of our private preoccupations and letting that world impose new senses on old phrases.
>
> A theological student whom later I knew as a senior friend had committed himself to starting his ministry in the north of England when he received a very attractive invitation to join a teaching institution in South Wales instead. He did not feel able to withdraw from his commitments, but one day he read in Isaiah 43:6, "I will say to the north, Give up" (Authorized Version), and concluded that this was God telling him that he would be providentially released from his promise and so set free to accept the second invitation.
>
> No such thing happened, however, so he went north after all, wondering what had gone wrong. Then he reread Isaiah 43:6 and noticed that it continued, "and to the south, Do not withhold." At this point it dawned on him that he had been finding meaning in the text that was never really there. Instead, the concerns which he brought to his reading of the text had governed his interpretation of it.
>
> To impose meaning on the text is not the way to learn God's Law. Yet we constantly do this (don't we?), and it is one chronic obstacle to understanding.[5]

I'm sure you've heard of people who make decisions by opening the Bible and randomly pointing to a verse and using it to make their choice. That's a foolish use of the Scriptures. God wants us to study the Word—the whole Bible, gleaning the principles we find and applying them to our decisions. That is how we derive accurate meaning from Scripture.

The issue of Bible context is multifaceted. It includes considerations, such as historical context, geographical context, and literary context.

Historical Context

When considering the historical context or setting, ask these kinds of questions:

- When did this happen?
- Where does this story, event, or teaching fit into the flow of history?
- What was going on politically, socially, and religiously at the time of the author's writing?

For example, 2 Kings 6 records the story of the miracle of a floating ax head. The miracle is impressive enough, showing God's power to do an unimaginable thing. But the miracle takes on further meaning when it is seen in its historical context. The story takes place during a volatile time in Israel's history, during the reign of Jehoram, the son of Ahab, whose evil reign as king of Israel plunged the nation headlong into destruction and captivity. At the time the man lost his ax in the river, Israel was about to go to war against the king of Aram. Yet on the eve of war and in the face of a coming national disaster, God mercifully performs a miracle to recover a borrowed ax that a man had inadvertently dropped into the river. Seen in its historical context, the miracle shows us a compassionate God who is willing to meet our most personal needs.

Geographical Context

Understanding the geographical setting of a passage of Scripture can aid us in discovering its full meaning. For example, Revelation 3:14-21 records Christ's message to the church at Laodicea—the lukewarm church. John writes the words of Jesus: "I know all the things you do, that you are neither hot nor cold. I wish that you were one or the other! But since you are like lukewarm water, neither hot nor cold, I will spit you out of my mouth!" (3:15-16).

The words "cold" and "hot" are familiar to everyone. But did you know that "cold" refers to the cold waterfalls of nearby Colossae, where thirsty travelers stopped for a refreshing drink? And did you know that "hot" refers to the hot springs of adjacent Hierapolis, where people soaked their bodies in an effort to eliminate their aches and pains? Jesus's warning is now better understood. Because believers at Laodicea have neither shared the refreshing drink of the gospel nor reached others with the healing power of Christ, they shall be disciplined.

Textual Context

We must see a verse in the context of a passage, a passage within a chapter, a chapter within a book, and a book within the whole Bible. What happens before and after a particular story or teaching? Does what precedes a text affect our interpretation of it?

Matthew 17:14-20 records Jesus's healing of an epileptic boy. Jesus says to His disciples, "You don't have enough faith...I tell you the truth, if you had faith even as small as a mustard seed, you could say to this mountain, 'Move from here to there,' and it would move. Nothing would be impossible" (Matthew 17:20). What mountain is Jesus referring to? The answer is found at the beginning of the chapter, which speaks of a "high mountain" on which Christ was transfigured (see Matthew 17:1). The point is that mountaintop experiences with God are meant to build faith, but they may start out as something as seemingly small and insignificant as a mustard seed.

Key 5: Understand the Ways God Speaks

The revelation of Scripture comes to us through diverse literary genres or forms. Each of these forms is normally read and understood somewhat differently. Just as we read a newspaper differently from how we read a novel, we need to read the Gospels' narratives differently from how we read the books of Old Testament law. Understanding literary forms will aid our understanding of various parts of the Scriptures. The Bible uses a variety of literary forms:

- *History*—Recounts God's mighty deeds in the past
- *Prophecy*—Reveals the future through messages from God
- *Psalms*—Present a wide range of truths from a human vantage point by using the medium of song and poetry
- *Proverbs*—Provide direction through sayings and adages that embody wisdom and truth
- *Narrative*—Reports and comments about unfolding events
- *Parables*—Teach universal truths using familiar settings as metaphors
- *Teaching*—Applies the holy character of God to how we should live

In addition to using a variety of literary genres, the Bible also uses literary devices, such as figures of speech. The Bible always speaks the absolute truth of God. However, some areas of the Bible are allegorical or figurative, while others are not. Here is an important Bible interpretation principle: *You should always take the literal meaning of a word or passage unless there is an overriding reason why you should interpret it figuratively.* If the Bible says, "The sheep are grazing on the hillside," you would interpret this literally, picturing a pastoral scene. But if the Bible says, "You are like sheep," you would recognize a figure of speech and look for what truth can be found in the comparison.

The Bible contains definite types of figurative language, including metaphor, simile, hyperbole, and anthropomorphism.

A *metaphor* uses a direct comparison: Something is something else. In John 15:1, Jesus states, "I am the true grapevine." This does not mean He is a literal grapevine but that He is the central figure from which His people, the branches, gain their life and nourishment. When Jesus changed Simon's name, He said, "Now I say to you that you are Peter (which means 'rock'), and upon this rock I will build my church, and all the powers of hell will not conquer it" (Matthew 16:18). To the people listening in to the conversation, Jesus was saying to Peter, "You are a rock." Did He mean the disciple was etched out of granite? No, Jesus was using a metaphor, suggesting that Peter would provide an unshakable foundation on which Jesus would build His church. The metaphor effectively communicated a deeper, fuller meaning.

A *simile* is a comparison using the words *like* or *as*. Exodus 24:17 states, "The glory of the LORD appeared at the summit like a consuming fire." This comparison—God's glory and a consuming fire—helps us to see aspects of God's glory more clearly.

A *hyperbole* is an exaggeration for emphasis. In John 21:25 we find an example of this: "Jesus also did many other things. If they were all written down, I suppose the whole world could not contain the books that would be written." We realize that the statement is made to emphasize the amount of ministry that Jesus accomplished when He was here on this earth.

An *anthropomorphism* is a figure of speech that attributes human characteristics—including body parts, humanlike actions, and even human emotions—to God. The Lord is said to have eyes: "Noah found favor in the eyes of the LORD" (Genesis 6:8 NIV). In one of God's messages to Job, He says: "They will see God's face and shout for joy" (Job 33:26 NIV). God does not have a literal face, but the figure of speech helps us to understand that God's relationship with His people is so intimate that it is as if we can see His face. And God was said to have hair and a head:

> I watched as thrones were put in place
>   and the Ancient One sat down to judge.
> His clothing was as white as snow,
>   his hair like whitest wool.
>   (Daniel 7:9)

Yet we know that God is spirit and is not limited by a physical body. But these word pictures help us relate to God in a way we can understand.

Key 6: Uncover Word Meanings

The Bible was mainly written in two languages that are foreign to most people: Hebrew (Old Testament) and Greek (New Testament). Not only do these languages function differently from English, but also many Hebrew and Greek words flow from Hebrew and Greek cultures. To understand the full meaning of many words in our English translations, we must understand the original Hebrew and Greek words used in the biblical text.

Although good translations of the Bible will provide the corresponding English word, there is often more behind a word than what a translation can offer. You will find help understanding the meaning of the original languages with tools such as a Bible dictionary, a Bible encyclopedia, and even Hebrew and Greek lexicons.

For example, Luke 24:13-49 records Jesus's interaction with His disciples after He had risen from the dead. He reminds His followers, "This is what is written: The Messiah will suffer and rise from the dead on the third day, and repentance for the forgiveness of sins will be preached in his name to all nations, beginning at Jerusalem" (24:46-47 NIV). What is Christ's message of repentance?

Repentance is not a word we use in everyday conversation, so it may help to check another resource to understand what the word means in the original language. If you were to consult, for example, a good resource on New Testament Greek, you would find that the English word *repentance* is translated from the Greek word *metanoia*. This is a compound word: *meta* means "a change" and *noia* means "knowledge."[6] In other words, God calls us to change our thinking, to make a 180-degree change in direction, which starts with our thoughts and leads to our lifestyle. Understanding the depths of meaning in the Greek word leaves no doubt about what Jesus was asking His followers to do.

You may be thinking, *Dictionaries, encyclopedias, and lexicons? Bible study is beginning to sound pretty hard.* Please do not misinterpret my remarks. Although the Bible is the greatest book ever written, full of ancient history, supernatural truth, and multilayered teachings, it is also to be read and understood like any other book. Do not think you need to spend many hours with Bible study tools or hire a professional to understand its message. The Bible is written using normal language, and it is to be read and interpreted according to the normal rules of grammar. However, Bible-study tools can serve to *enhance* your understanding of Scripture and *assist* you in case you get stuck on a difficult passage.

There are many fine Bible helps, including Bible dictionaries, handbooks, commentaries, concordances, lexical aids, encyclopedias, and books on biblical theology that highlight the importance of Scripture.

My Favorite Way to Learn

While I use Bible-study tools in my study of Scripture, my preferred approach is simply to read, meditate, and reread. Before I read, I begin...

With prayer. I say, "Lord, what is it You want to say to me in this passage? Holy Spirit of God, You inspired your prophets and apostles to record these holy truths. Illumine my mind so that I can understand what You want me to know as I read." The Holy Spirit then calls my attention to things that are especially relevant. As I turn to the page, I read...

With reverence. For many years I began and ended each day reading the Bible while kneeling. Health complications have made kneeling and standing somewhat difficult, so I have had to reflect my reverence internally rather than externally. Reading with reverence truly brings the meaning of Scripture alive. Unless we read the Bible in submission to the Holy Spirit and in a spirit of respect and worship before almighty God, we will not understand what He wants to say to us from His inspired Word.

DISCOVER THE TREASURE

In this chapter I have shared some keys to study the Bible. One of them is observation. Here and in the next two chapters, I want you to use observation to discover something about yourself as well as the treasures in God's Word.

As I read my Bible each day, I find that I observe some passages only casually, but others prompt me to use more careful observation. Try to use this deeper level of observation in this study.

To begin, ask the Holy Spirit to guide you in your study. Then read the following passage about the Great Commandment at least twice, and answer the questions based on your personal observations. For the rest of the studies in this book, I encourage you to use a notebook in which to write down your thoughts. You may want to write some prayer points that relate to what you have learned or to what the Spirit is prompting you to do. This is a wonderful way to realize just how precious the illumination of the Holy Spirit can be.

> Read Matthew 22:34-40.

Observation Questions:

1. What does this passage teach me about God's character?

2. What command should I obey?

3. What does this passage teach about life's priorities?

4. How does this passage direct my faith?

5. What in my life do I need to change to respond appropriately to the passage's teaching?

6. What is the purpose of the text?

> Prayer Points:

7

How Do I Apply Bible-Study Principles?

Have you ever faced a situation that was so unsettling that your passions took over your actions? What happened as a result? Did you do the right thing, or did you make your situation worse and face harsh consequences?

Amerigo Munigia was a troubled man. He described himself this way: "I was always very violent, always wanting to fight with everybody." Finally, his situation in his home country of El Salvador became so dangerous for him that his name was placed on a guerilla hit list. Frightened, he took his wife and five children and fled to Los Angeles in 1981.

After the family was settled into their new home, Amerigo's oldest son, Juan, began attending a church and accepted Christ as his Savior. He told his dad what he had done, and Amerigo eventually became a Christian too.

As a new believer, Amerigo met with two of our Campus Crusade staff members for Bible study and Christian training. They encouraged him to live for Christ in every situation. Amerigo's life began to change for the better.

Sometime later, Juan saw three gangsters attack a street preacher. Juan came to the preacher's aid and fought the attackers, chasing them off. Three days later, the gangsters assassinated Juan by shooting him three times in the head.

When Amerigo saw his son lying bloodied and lifeless in the street, his violent feelings surged. He says, "At that moment, I wanted to be the man I used to be and retaliate."

From a friend, Amerigo found out where the gangsters were hiding. He grabbed a handgun and headed for the apartment building. His wife, Margarita, saw him going out the door and asked, "What is going on? You can't do that."

He didn't listen. His mind was so full of rage that he vowed he would return violence for violence.

He and his friend jumped into his friend's car and sped toward the apartment building. As the friend drove, the Holy Spirit began to work in Amerigo's heart. He recalled a verse in Scripture: "Do not take revenge, my dear friends, but leave room for God's wrath, for it is written: 'It is mine to avenge; I will repay,' says the Lord" (Romans 12:19 NIV). It was as if God said to him, "You do not have to do what you are going to do. You have to treat them with love."

He threw down the gun and asked his friend to drop him off at the apartment building. When he walked inside the apartment, the gangsters recognized him and reached for their weapons.

Quietly Amerigo explained to the men that he was not there to harm them. He told them about the love of Jesus Christ. Miraculously, the gangsters who had murdered his son prayed to receive Jesus as their Savior.[7]

Amerigo's actions are an example of the miracles that can happen when we apply the Bible in every aspect of our will and emotions. With the help of other believers, Amerigo had learned basic passages in the Bible and how to apply them to his life. He committed himself to obeying the Word to please God. Then when he was faced with a crisis in which his emotions threatened to take him down the wrong path, the verses he had learned helped him choose to do the right thing. The Holy Spirit used the Bible to show him how to respond.

Whether you are involved in a crisis right now or are living in one of those rare times of peace, applying God's Word is what will transform you from a reactor to an actor on God's stage.

The Growth Principle

The truths of the Word of God have the power to change our lives. But how does that happen? Jesus told a parable that illustrates the interrelationship of Christian growth and God's Word. We can use the lessons from the parable as we study the Bible.

> "Listen! A farmer went out to plant some seeds. As he scattered them across his field, some seeds fell on a footpath, and the birds came and ate them. Other seeds fell on shallow soil with underlying rock. The seeds sprouted quickly because the soil was shallow. But the plants soon wilted under the hot sun, and since they didn't have deep roots, they died. Other seeds fell among thorns that grew up and choked out the tender plants. Still other seeds fell on fertile soil, and they produced a crop that was thirty, sixty, and even a hundred times as much as had been planted! Anyone with ears to hear should listen and understand" (Matthew 13:3-9).

The disciples were mystified about the meaning of this story. Then Jesus offered this explanation:

> "The seed that fell on the footpath represents those who hear the message about the Kingdom and don't understand it. Then the evil one comes and snatches away the seed that was planted in their hearts. The seed on the rocky soil represents those who hear the message and immediately receive it with joy. But since they don't have deep roots, they don't last long. They fall away as soon as they have problems or are persecuted for believing God's word. The seed that fell among the thorns represents those who hear God's word, but all too quickly the message is crowded out by the worries of this life and the lure of wealth, so no fruit is produced. The seed that fell on good soil represents those who truly hear and understand God's word and produce a harvest of thirty, sixty, or even a hundred times as much as had been planted!" (Matthew 13:19-23).

The parable illustrates that the seed—the Good News, the Word of God, God's message—grows and becomes productive only when the conditions of the soil are right. Jesus was asking His listeners to think about their own lives. Were they rocky soil? Thorny ground? Good soil?

The parable asks the same of us today. What kind of soil are you? Are you rocky soil, hearing the truth in the Bible but not letting it take root in your life? Are you thorny soil, hearing and accepting God's message in His Word but not giving it priority? Or are you good soil, not only hearing and accepting the truths of the Bible but also applying it to every life situation? Clearly, Jesus wants us to be like the good soil: open, responsive, productive, and fruitful.

Application and Change

When we apply God's Word, we will see specific changes in our lives. As a young believer, I enrolled in Princeton Theological Seminary and later Fuller Theological Seminary. For five years I sat at the feet of some of the most learned and godly theologians of the last century. Although I learned many wonderful things during those years, I was most profoundly influenced by the constant teaching on the supernatural authority of the inerrant Word of God. If only we can comprehend the incredible riches of this God-inspired book, the Bible, our lives will never be the same.

God does not come into our lives with His supernatural and inerrant Word so that we can continue to live as we want in our self-centered pleasure. He comes to radically change us. His purpose is to transform us into men and women with hearts on fire for God. But this will happen only as we live out what He has shown us. When we do, our faithfulness will shine so that others will see our change and come to know the wonderful truth of forgiveness of sins and the abundant life that He offers—just as it did in the life of Amerigo Munigia.

God wants to create change in several areas of our lives through His Word.

1. God uses His Word to make us like Jesus, our marvelous Lord and Savior. As we read the Scriptures and come to know the character of

God and His Son, Jesus Christ, we are drawn to be more like Him. We see Jesus's humility, and we are drawn to be humble. We see Jesus's servant heart, and we are drawn to serve others. We see Jesus's obedience to His Father's will, and we are drawn to obey God's will. God accomplishes this kind of growth in holiness through a process theologians call sanctification.

2. God's Word opens our hearts to the truth of God's holy nature. If you have walked along a wilderness path at night, you understand how important your flashlight becomes. Without it, you would trip over roots hidden in the shadows, be afraid of every sound coming from the underbrush, and perhaps even lose your way. But the light allows you to walk on with confident strides. That is similar to how God's Word becomes a light for us. It leads us to purity and righteousness. The psalmist declares, "Your word is a lamp to guide my feet and a light for my path" (Psalm 119:105). The Bible leads us to the light and helps us to grow and change in ways that please God.

3. God changes us by revealing His will through His Word. Most believers want to follow the will of God, but they are not always certain what that will is. The Bible is very clear about God's will in the phrases I've italicized in verses such as these:

> *Don't worry* about anything; instead, *pray* about everything. *Tell God what you need,* and *thank him* for all he has done (Philippians 4:6).

> So *stop telling lies.* Let us *tell our neighbors the truth,* for we are all parts of the same body. And *"don't sin by letting anger control you." Don't let the sun go down while you are still angry,* for anger gives a foothold to the devil.
>
> If you are a thief, *quit stealing.* Instead, *use your hands for good hard work,* and then *give generously to others in need. Don't use foul or abusive language. Let everything you say be good and helpful,* so that your words will be an encouragement to those who hear them (Ephesians 4:25-29).

But sometimes God's will is not so clear. Should you take a certain job? Should you move to another state? As you pray for God's Holy Spirit to lead you and as you search the Scriptures, I am confident He will show you His will. I offer this word of caution: Remember that if something is truly God's will, it needs to line up with the *whole* of the Bible's teaching.

I refer to a passage mentioned in the last chapter, where Satan tempted Jesus in the wilderness. Satan used words from the Scriptures to try to convince Jesus to obey him. But as we saw earlier, Jesus knew that Satan was using just a fragment of the Scriptures to distort God's will. Jesus knew the whole of Scripture, so He quoted a verse back: "The Scriptures also say, 'You must not test the LORD your God'" (Matthew 4:7).

Jesus was quick to see through Satan's clever ploy. Christ's response to Satan proves that although the devil's point lined up with one part of Scripture, it did not line up with the whole of it. Jesus could see all of Scripture as one message, one spirit, and one unity. We must do the same as we try to determine what God wants in our lives. Some decisions will be easy; others will take deeper consideration, prayer, and knowing the whole of God's Word.

4. God's Word changes us by allowing us to experience the very life of God. The Christianity I knew as a young believer was hardly characterized by the supernatural. Although I was exposed to good, solid, fundamental Bible teaching, there was little emphasis on the supernatural. So when I first heard the promise from Jeremiah 33:3—"Call to me and I will answer you and tell you great and unsearchable things you do not know" (NIV)—I was challenged. What did it mean? How could I personally experience a quality of life that is obviously superior to anything that I was then experiencing or that others around me were experiencing?

As I prayed for the fulfillment of God's promise to reveal "great and unsearchable things," He began to show me His own supernatural resources that are available to every believer. I began to understand the mighty attributes of God—His holiness, sovereignty, love, wisdom, power, grace, and compassion. I began to realize, and have experienced again and again through the years, the revolutionary meaning of "Christ in you, the hope of glory" (Colossians 1:27 NIV).

This is one of the most important lessons that any believer can learn—that with Christ in us we are no longer ordinary, mediocre human beings. But when we receive Christ, we embrace the life of the infinite creator God, who possesses all the unlimited supernatural resources we need to help us live godly lives and to be fruitful witnesses. This can be possible only as we study and apply God's Word in our hearts and lives.

Why Don't We Grow?

I've heard people say, "I study the Word, yet it hasn't produced change in me. What's wrong?"

Many times people apply the Word in wrong ways. This is easy to do. The great Bible teacher Howard G. Hendricks and his son Bill offer four insights about this issue in their book *Living by the Book*.[8]

1. We substitute interpretation for application. We've all done this from time to time. We study a passage that's fascinating to us and begin to dig deeper and deeper. But what we are mining are just facts, and our lives do not change. I'm sure you've been part of a group that was more interested in interpreting the Scriptures than applying them. Each week brought more discussion but no life changes. We must make sure that our goal in Bible study is to see what God is telling us personally, not what we can learn to fill our minds. In this situation we are like the rocky ground. We allow biblical truth to penetrate only the surface of our lives.

2. We substitute superficial obedience for substantive life change. Oh, how easy this is to do—and to not recognize we are doing it. We read the words "do not worry" in Matthew 6:25 (NIV), and we occasionally catch ourselves, but we go on living with daily, sometimes debilitating anxiety. We agree with Ephesians 4:27 that our anger gives a foothold to Satan, and we stop shouting at our children. But we still seethe each time an irritating situation arises with them. God sees our hearts. He knows if our obedience is superficial or if our hearts have been changed. We must tend the soil of our lives so that God's Word can touch the deepest parts of our hearts and create change.

3. *We substitute rationalization for repentance.* No matter how we describe it, conviction is not pleasant. When the Holy Spirit convicts us of sin, our first reaction is to excuse ourselves. When we read the words in Ephesians 4:28, "If you are a thief, quit stealing," we dismiss them as words aimed at criminals who steal from banks. We conclude that those words don't apply to us. But what about some of our work practices? How easy it is to rationalize our own stealing. We say, "My employer owes me something for the hard work I do, so she won't mind if I take off a little early to do some errands without noting that on my time sheet." If she doesn't mind, why not ask her? We can find so many ways to make light of our sin. When God's Word zeros in on a sinful area in our lives, we need to fall before Him in sorrow and repent of our actions. That's the attitude that brings about change and pleases God.

4. *We substitute an emotional decision for a volitional decision.* How many times have you come across a Scripture passage that directly points out a sin or a change that you know God wants you to make, and you respond with only your emotions? Perhaps you read in James 3:5-6 (NIV),

> The tongue is a small part of the body, but it makes great boasts. Consider what a great forest is set on fire by a small spark. The tongue also is a fire, a world of evil among the parts of the body. It corrupts the whole body, sets the whole course of one's life on fire, and is itself set on fire by hell.

You know that Scripture is speaking to you. So you pray with deep emotion that you want God to make a change in your life. But when you close your Bible and go on with your daily routine, you forget all about your decision. You have responded at the moment with emotions but have not responded with your will by your commitment to carry out the change.

Each of these insights describes soil that is rocky or thorny. We hear the truth of the Word, but it doesn't take root in our lives. We must pray, asking the Holy Spirit to cultivate the soil of our hearts so that we will have the courage and strength to *do* the will of God, not just *hear* it.

> But don't just listen to God's word. You must do what it says. Otherwise, you are only fooling yourselves. For if you listen to the word and don't obey, it is like glancing at your face in a mirror. You see yourself, walk away, and forget what you look like. But if you look carefully into the perfect law that sets you free, and if you do what it says and don't forget what you heard, then God will bless you for doing it (James 1:22-25).

Be aware of the blessings and power He gives you to apply what you find in His Word. For the difficult areas that you have problems controlling, ask a friend to help you be accountable or to study the Bible with you. Having a spiritual brother or sister walk alongside you can make the difference in your heart's obedience.

Steps to Application

To help you apply what you learn, take the following three steps during your Bible study.

1. Study with a willing heart. Before you read the Bible, ask God to prepare your heart for what He has to say to you. Tell Him that you will listen for His voice as you read and that you will commit to doing what He tells you.

2. Examine yourself. That's basically what James is telling us in the verses above. The Scripture will point out areas that we need to apply to our lives, but we must examine our routine, experiences, temptations, and opportunities to see how God wants us to apply what we learn.

3. Meditate on God's Word. Meditation is an art that few Christians practice today. When is the last time you spent extra time letting God's Word soak through your mind, asking Him to use it to heal you and change you? This is not emptying our mind but filling it with God's Word. Take time out in your day to really think about what God is saying to you.

DISCOVER THE TREASURE

How was your observation with the last Discover the Treasure section? Did you find yourself recalling during the day the passage you studied?

In this chapter I detailed some keys to Bible-study application:

- Study with a willing heart.
- Examine yourself.
- Meditate on God's Word.

Use these keys during your observation of the passage listed at the end of these instructions. Remember to write your responses in your Bible-study notebook.

The first key relates to the attitude you bring to your study. Make sure it is pleasing to God. The second key encourages you to open yourself to the Holy Spirit's conviction or prompting as you study. If you don't allow the Spirit to illumine your life, your study will not be effective. The third key is what you can do after your study. This is where Bible memorization becomes so important. Memorize the verse that you think is key, or write it on a card to keep with you during the day and meditate on it.

Now use your observation skills to study the following passage about spreading God's message. Be sure to write down prayer points as they occur to you.

Read Colossians 1:24-29.

Observation Questions:

1. What does this passage teach me about God's character?
2. What does this passage teach me about Jesus Christ?
3. What does this passage teach me about how I should live?
4. How does this passage direct my faith?

5. What command or promise should I obey or claim?

6. What in my life do I need to change to respond appropriately to the passage's teaching?

7. What is the purpose of the text?

Prayer Points:

8

How Can I Strengthen My Commitment to Bible Study?

At age forty, Jeff is a successful businessperson, the head of a multi-million-dollar company. But when people ask Jeff what gives him satisfaction, he doesn't talk about his work or his company. He talks about his children. And the Bible.

God's Word is so important in Jeff's life that he has begun a rigorous discipline with his wife and three children, ages seven through twelve. They have committed to reading through the Bible in a year—together. Each night they gather to hear Jeff or his wife, Janine, read aloud from the *One Year Bible*. But since Jeff wants to make sure that his children understand the Bible and its meaning for their lives, he has committed himself to studying each day's passages ahead of time and writing out notes that will help his children connect with some aspect of the passages. It's an enormous time commitment for Jeff, but he believes it is so important for his children to understand the Bible that he is willing to spend hours each day to ensure their growth. Even when he's traveling, Jeff maintains this discipline with his family. He calls home and joins the family by phone to maintain the family Bible study time.

What motivates Jeff and Janine? Their deep love for God, their love for their children, and their great respect for the power of God's Word to shape and direct our lives.

Kenneth Taylor was motivated by many of the same loves. Concerned that his ten children were not understanding the Bible when he read aloud from the King James Version at family mealtimes, Ken decided to do something about it. Every day while he commuted by train from his home in Wheaton, Illinois, to his job at Moody Press in Chicago, he took his Bible and wrote out a restatement of each verse of the passage he would read to his family that evening. He was so encouraged by his family's response that he continued his exercise until he had paraphrased whole books of the Bible. As some of you know, that discipline was the beginning of *The Living Bible*.[9]

These people and their families have committed themselves to daily Bible reading and study because they have a hunger to know God, to understand what His will is for their lives, and to ground the lives of their families in that will and Word. If you asked them, each of them would tell you that studying the Bible is the most important work of their lives.

Many of you would like to have that same experience—and you can. By now you have learned a few tools for reading, studying, and understanding the Bible, and the remaining chapters of this book will equip you with even more. I hope that you are catching a glimpse of the power of the Bible to help you discover who God is and how much He loves you. I encourage you to make a long-term commitment to make Bible reading and study an essential part of your life. That discipline is built one day at a time.

A Commitment to God's Word

We all agree about our need for Bible study. But sometimes the daily grind of life discourages us from keeping our commitment. When that happens, I often find encouragement from the stories of how others approached their study of God's Word. I'd like to share some of those stories with you in the hope that when your enthusiasm flags or you are tired from your hectic day, you can recall one of these accounts and be inspired to keep your commitment fresh.

Billy Sunday

One of the most influential Christians in American history started out as a major-league baseball player. He was born in a small town in Iowa in the late 1800s and was known for his drinking and betting. In spite of the ridicule of his colleagues, he turned his life over to Jesus Christ after hearing the Pacific Garden Mission group singing gospel hymns. That decision was the pivot point of his life.

His name was Billy Sunday, and he played baseball for four more years after his conversion. Then he began working for God full-time as a preacher and evangelist.

Over the next twenty-five years, Billy Sunday delivered the message of hope in Jesus Christ about twenty thousand times. It is estimated that two million people received Christ as their Savior because of his ministry. In one ten-week campaign in New York City alone, a million and a half people came to the meetings.[10]

And all this from a small-town boy who gave up what most Americans considered a dream job in the major leagues. Yet Billy Sunday's life was dedicated to something higher—to God's Word. This beautiful inscription was found in his Bible:

> Twenty-nine years ago, with the Holy Spirit as my Guide, I entered at the portico of Genesis, walked down the corridor of the Old Testament art galleries, where pictures of Noah, Abraham, Moses, Joseph, Isaac, Jacob, and Daniel hung on the wall. I passed into the music room of the Psalms where the Spirit sweeps the keyboard of nature until it seems that every reed and pipe in God's great organ responds to the harp of David, the sweet singer of Israel.
>
> I entered the chamber of Ecclesiastes, where the voice of the preacher is heard, and into the conservatory of Sharon and the lily of the valley where sweet spices filled and perfumed my life.
>
> I entered into the business office of Proverbs and on into the observatory of the prophets, where I saw telescopes of various sizes pointing to far-off events, concentrating on the bright and morning Star, which was to rise above the moonlit hills of Judea for our salvation and redemption.
>
> I entered the audience room of the King of kings, catching a vision written by Matthew, Mark, Luke, and John.

Thence into the correspondence room with Paul, Peter, and John writing their Epistles.

I stepped into the throne room of Revelation, where tower the glittering peaks, where sits the King of kings upon His throne of glory with the healing of nations in His hand, and I cried out:

All hail the power of Jesus' name.
Let angels prostrate fall;
Bring forth the royal diadem
And crown Him Lord of all.[11]

He expressed the scope of what we will experience when we practice consistent and meaningful Bible study. We will find amazing stories, truths, blessings, promises, and treasures in all its pages. Our lives will take on a new dimension.

The Desert Monks

In every generation God raises up people who have a single-minded focus on Him. More than seventeen centuries ago, some men dedicated themselves to becoming more like God. They didn't want just to study about God—they wanted their lives to mirror God's image. They practiced their faith by renouncing material possessions and living a humble life in the desert. Church history refers to these men as the desert monks. Obedience to God's Word was one of their hallmarks.

What is so fascinating about their lifestyle is that they constantly meditated on Scripture. For example, they chanted Scripture passages as they wove their baskets. One monk, Abba Ammonius, is credited with memorizing the entire Old and New Testaments.[12] Their strength was in their disciplined life. They were able to put aside temporal desires, such as the pull to own material possessions and the enticement of ungodly passions, to concentrate on serving God wholeheartedly.

In our world filled with advertisements, entertainment, and illicit passions, the desert monks stand as a wonderful example of our need to discipline ourselves to know and apply God's Word. We don't have to isolate ourselves in the desert like they did to serve Him, but we can have the heart of these monks toward disciplining ourselves to study God's Word.

Dwight L. Moody

How could a salesman who had only a fourth-grade education leave such a far-reaching influence? He was a tireless evangelist who reached millions with the gospel, founded numerous schools, including Moody Bible Institute, and started two publishing companies: Fleming H. Revell and Moody Press. During his lifetime, Dwight L. Moody probably traveled more than one million miles and preached to more than one hundred million people. And that was in the days of sooty train travel and rough, unpaved roads.[13]

Because of his background, Moody was never a great student, and he didn't spend time puzzling over deep theological issues. He considered the Bible as a commonplace book in this sense: he believed that anyone could study it and it would change that person's heart. He also believed that a Christian had to approach Bible study with the right spirit and effort. He said, "Study and work go hand in hand."[14] He was a great supporter of Sunday schools, and in his classrooms, he coordinated knowledge with actual experience.

What can we gain from Moody's example? He was an ordinary man with less than stellar academic qualifications, and yet God used him in a mighty way. Moody didn't let what was missing in his background keep him from knowing the Bible. He transferred his commitment to Bible study with accompanying application to millions of others through his Sunday schools. Even today, the educational institutions he founded are still training believers in God's Word.

We also can take what God has given us in our background and education and study God's Word. All God asks is that we use what He has given us in His service.

Charles Wesley

Perhaps you have heard of John Wesley, founder of the Methodist denomination. Less famous is his beloved brother Charles, who is considered the greatest hymn writer of all ages. I'm sure you've sung some of his hymns: "Hark! The Herald Angels Sing," "O for a Thousand Tongues to Sing," "And Can It Be," or "Love Divine, All Loves Excelling." Where did he get his inspiration for his verses? His mind was steeped in God's Word.

It all began in 1738, when Charles Wesley became ill. At the time, he was staying with friends in London. While he was in bed, he heard a voice telling him to believe in the name of Jesus. He got out of bed, opened his Bible, and read. Right there he found peace with God.

Two days later he penned his first hymn. The next day he showed it to his brother, who had also received Christ as Savior. John was impressed, so he and other friends stood beside Charles's bed and sang the new hymn of praise to God. That was the beginning of the hymn-writing career of Charles Wesley.

Frank Bohr says of Charles Wesley's verses, "[They are] an enormous sponge, filled to saturation with Bible words, Bible similes, Bible metaphors, Bible stories, and Bible themes."[15]

What can we learn from Charles Wesley? Through Bible study, God will fill our souls with joy and song. We may never achieve hymn-writing fame, but we will have an abundance of praise for our Lord.

Taking the Step

I could tell many other stories of how Bible study affected people's lives. But right now, I encourage you to make your own commitment to Bible study by following four simple steps that will help you keep your focus on God and His Word.

1. In prayer, commit yourself to Bible study. We need to rely on God's strength to help us grow in our spirits. We can never do it on our own. Therefore, the first step is to call on Him and tell Him about your desire to be immersed in His Word. God is not interested in flowery words, so make your request simple and heartfelt. Write down the time and the date so that you can look back to this decision as the starting point in your journey in God's Word.

Also, at this time decide when and where you will study and how long your study will last. It's important to set a starting and ending time, or you may get so involved in your study that time gets away from you. After several long study times, your enthusiasm may wane. To avoid that possibility, limit your study times. A half an hour a week is a good beginning point. Later, as you see how you work, you can adjust the time.

2. *Renew your commitment each morning.* As I have mentioned, Vonette and I study our Bibles each morning. It is at this time that I dedicate my day to our wonderful Lord. This helps me to keep myself in line with my commitment. I ask God to make me His vessel for the day and to remind me of what His Word says and how I need to apply it.

3. *Plan your day to carry out your commitment.* Since you may not be doing actual Bible study each day, plan to include some of what you are learning in your study in the days you don't include Bible study. For example, if you set aside an hour for study on Monday, keep the verses and truths you learn clearly in mind so that they become a part of your routine the rest of the days. You might want to write down these verses and truths on index cards and slip them into your Bible as a reminder. Read them during your morning prayer time.

4. *Prepare for the time when you will be tempted to fail—or when you do fail—in your commitment.* Many people get discouraged when they do not follow through in their commitments to God, and they often give up on the commitment entirely. Inevitably, you will face times when you will not feel well, will have a bad day, or will be tempted to abandon your commitment. These times will come, but they are not insurmountable. It is at these times that it is most important to renew your commitment and return to God's Word with renewed vigor.

Now that we have covered the essentials of why we believe the Bible and how we can understand it, we can move on to another area: What is the Bible about? We learned that the central Person of the Bible is Jesus Christ, but that is just the beginning of our discovery concerning our awesome God. In part 3 we will find out how the Bible describes God. That's a fascinating and glorious study.

DISCOVER THE TREASURE

For your study this time, I have included two passages. Each tells of a time when the apostle Paul went to a synagogue and told people about Jesus. An important part of observation is being able to compare one passage with another. Do this study in three parts:

1. Study the first passage by reading it and answering the observation questions.

2. Study the second passage by reading it and answering the same observation questions.

3. Compare the two passages by using the "Compare" questions at the bottom of the observation question list. See how much more you can find in two passages by comparing them.

Also, remember the four steps of commitment to Bible study:

1. In prayer, commit yourself to Bible study.

2. Renew your commitment each morning.

3. Plan to carry out your commitment.

4. Prepare for the time when you will be tempted to fail—or when you do fail—in your commitment.

Now use your observation skills to study the following two passages. Write your observations in your notebook, and be sure to write down prayer points as they occur to you.

Read Acts 17:1-9 and Acts 17:10-15.

Observation Questions (use the same questions for both passages):

1. What is the most important truth in this passage?

2. What does this passage teach me about God's nature?

3. What does this passage teach me about life's priorities?

4. How does this passage relate to me?

5. What do I need to change in my life to conform it to the passage's teaching?

6. What is the purpose of the text?

Compare:

1. What do the two passages have in common?

2. What similar reactions do I have to the two passages?

3. What different reactions do I have to the two passages?

4. Which of the characters in the passages would I most want to be like? Why?

Prayer Points:

PART 3

What Is the Bible About?

*"The study of God is not only the most meaningful
and the most authentic pursuit in life, it is also the
most beneficial. Nothing will benefit you more in
day-to-day living than the knowledge of God."*

Tony Evans

9

Our Powerful Creator

Come and take a whirlwind tour around the universe with me. First, we'll travel into outer space through the eye of the Hubble telescope.

Hubble's gaze turns toward what seems like the emptiest part of space. But instead of a void, we see layers and layers of galaxies as far as the telescope can reach. And within each galaxy are billions of stars.

Slowly, the Hubble eye turns toward a large planet. It's Saturn, and we note a huge storm resembling a white arrowhead spread over the planet's equator. Saturn's rings are sharply defined. As Hubble continues to show us the wonders of the heavens, our minds are stunned at the beauty and variety.[1]

Let's leave the telescope and fly over the Atlantic Ocean to investigate an underwater mountain range known as the Mid-Atlantic Ridge. We settle into a submersible craft for a trip two and a half miles under the seawater's surface. As we plunge into the depths, our eyes are fastened on the porthole.

The craft settles into a valley on the ocean floor. Except for the powerful headlight on the submersible, the area is dark at this depth. The light sweeps over huge billowing black clouds that threaten to obscure our view. We can feel a tremendous force trying to pull us into a large hole on the sea floor. We are witnessing the power of a deep-sea geyser with its 650-degree inferno.

In this dark, overheated world, we expect to find no life. But amazingly, we see billions of tiny eyeless shrimp teeming around the black chimney of the geyser. We learn that they are feeding on bacteria especially suited to this environment. As the light scans the water, we notice another odd creature the size of a silver dollar and resembling a Chinese checkerboard. It is nestled into the mineral chimneys built up from the spouting geyser.[2]

After we emerge from the sea floor, we continue our journey across the ocean to the shores of Brazil. In a short time we find ourselves floating on an air raft above the rain forest canopy.

As we settle back to enjoy the soft ride, all we can see below us for miles and miles is a sea of green—an ocean of leaves and branches. The air is soaked from the 155 inches of annual rainfall. The evaporation is so intense that it almost seems as if rain is falling up. The atmosphere is alive with sounds—monkey chatter, bird noises of all kinds, insects buzzing, and the croak of frogs. We see plants whose roots are used only for holding onto the trees. A beetle lands on the side of our raft; it is the size of a child's closed fist and its "horns" make its head look like the head of a rhinoceros.

Just when we get comfortable floating along in this unique world, we journey to a scientific laboratory, where the equipment can magnify small objects up to fifty thousand times. Through this new lens, we see yet another universe.

The microscope is programmed to let us see inside a living cell—the building block of all living things. We recall that Charles Darwin, who propagated the theory of evolution, called the cell a black box because in his day, no one had seen the inside of this structure. He thought that a cell was just a blob of protoplasm.

But as we zoom in on the round shape in front of us, we see how wrong Darwin was. Inside the cell are many little machinelike forms that are busy doing their specific tasks. One tiny "truck" is carrying material from one side of the cell to the other. Another, a gatekeeper, is part of the cell wall, and its job is to let good materials in and keep harmful ones out. Then we see the DNA, a ladderlike structure with innumerable rungs. This tiny bit of matter carries all the information needed to reproduce an exact replica of the cell.

As we examine one of the tiny structures, we notice that it is comprised of many smaller molecules. These are all proteins, and they are interlocked in a chain that makes up the form of the structure. Before our eyes, the chain unwinds so we can see how perfectly formed it is. The chain is made of a long line of amino acids. As it folds back up on itself, we see how it all fits together perfectly. We realize that each structure in the cell has its own unique chain and pattern of amino acids. What intricacy and wonder. This is no black box; it is a miniscule, complicated factory working on its own without a manager to guide it.[3]

Our trip has ended, and we are speechless at the wonders of what we saw. We realize that this glimpse is only a minute fraction of the universe and its intricate design.

The Great Designer

This is a glimpse at what God, our Creator, has done. As Christians, we realize that anything this intricate and detailed has to have a manager. And a designer. For example, any computer functions according to a design and contains highly coded information. We naturally attribute the origin of the computer's design to an intelligent designer. In fact, we assume that the more sophisticated the machine, the more sophisticated was the planning and forethought that went into its development. No one would suggest that something as complex and sophisticated as a computer happened by chance or by natural selection. This thought would be considered absurd.

So it is with life forms on earth. Life on earth is far more intricate than the most complex computer equipment. In fact, the collective genius of the most superior minds throughout human history has failed to produce a machine as sophisticated as the simplest replicating life form. The grand design of creation and the coded information contained within must be attributed to a designer whose aptitude and skills are vastly superior to those of humans.

The French mathematician Lecompte de Nouy examined the laws of probability, seeking to discover the odds that a single molecule of high dissymmetry could be formed by chance. De Nouy found that, on average, the time needed to form one such molecule of our terrestrial globe would be about 10^{253} (that's 10 followed by more than 250 zeros) billion years. (Can you even imagine that number?)

"But," continued de Nouy ironically, "let us admit that no matter how small the chance it could happen, one molecule could be created by such astronomical odds of chance. However, one molecule is of no use. Hundreds of millions of identical ones are necessary. Thus we either admit the miracle or doubt the absolute truth of science."[4]

Of course, the person who designed it all is God our Creator. From the billion-star galaxies to the bits of chemicals that make up our DNA, God's hand is evident.

The Bible tells us much about this God. We began to explore His nature in an earlier chapter, but now we will discover from the Scriptures just how awesome and perfect He is. In part 3 we will look at His abilities as the Creator, His integrity as the perfect judge, and His intimacy as our loving Savior.

The Testimony of the Astronauts

As we look at our created world, our eyes naturally turn to the Creator. The wonder of space is so overpowering that after the astronauts spent time in space, many of them developed a deep belief in God. In a *BreakPoint* radio commentary, Charles Colson describes the impact of space travel on several astronauts.

> American astronauts Neil Armstrong and Buzz Aldrin landed on the moon and took that "giant leap for mankind." But before they emerged from the spaceship, Aldrin slipped out a few items he had smuggled on board: a Bible, a silver chalice, and sacramental bread and wine. There on the moon, his first act was to celebrate communion. Aldrin is not the only astronaut who is deeply religious. For many astronauts, an unexpected result of their participation in the space program is to inspire or deepen their spiritual commitments.
>
> Frank Borman was commander of the first space crew to travel beyond the Earth's orbit. Looking down on the earth

from 250,000 miles in space, Borman radioed back a message, reading from Genesis 1: "In the beginning, God created the heavens and the earth." As he explained in a recent interview, "I had an enormous feeling that there had to be a power greater than any of us—that there was a God, that there was indeed a beginning."

James Irwin, who walked on the moon in 1971, later became an evangelical minister and founded a Baptist ministry. He often describes the lunar mission as a revelation. In his words, "I felt the power of God as I'd never felt it before."

Charles Duke, who followed Irwin to the moon, later became active in Christian missionary work. He has an Episcopal ministry and speaks frequently at religious gatherings around the country. As he puts it, "I make speeches about walking on the moon and walking with the Son"— the Son of God, that is.[5]

What is there about being in space that sparks an innate religious sense? Philosopher Immanuel Kant said there are two things that "fill the mind with ever new and increasing admiration and awe: the starry heavens above me and the moral law within me."[6]

Actually, the Bible explains this phenomenon:

The heavens proclaim the glory of God.
The skies display his craftsmanship.
Day after day they continue to speak;
night after night they make him known.
They speak without a sound or word;
their voice is never heard.
Yet their message has gone throughout the earth,
and their words to all the world.
(Psalm 19:1-4)

These verses poetically describe our reaction to the vastness and wonder of space. But what does the Bible say about all those tiny pieces of matter within a cell and about their ability to do all their tasks seemingly on their own? Hebrews 1:3 explains the Creator's relationship to His creation: "[The Son] sustains everything by the mighty power of his command." We can think of all the perfectly tuned machinery of the universe—from the billions of stars to the ocean creatures to the diversity of the rain forest to the minute particles that make up all living cells—as part of a vast army directed by God. It all flows and grows at the word of His design and His command.

The Testimony of the Bible

The message of the Bible is that God is the magnificent Creator who put so much beauty and diversity in every corner of the world that we can only stand in awe. What does the Bible say about God's abilities and power as Creator?

God Is Above the Universe

Have you ever heard people speak of God as if He is their buddy? While God is our friend, we must never forget that He is so much greater than we are. Look again at one of the Bible's pictures of our relationship to our heavenly Father:

> Haven't you heard? Don't you understand?
>   Are you deaf to the words of God—
> the words he gave before the world began?
>   Are you so ignorant?
> God sits above the circle of the earth.
>   The people below seem like grasshoppers to him!
> He spreads out the heavens like a curtain
>   and makes his tent from them.
> He judges the great people of the world
>   and brings them all to nothing.
> They hardly get started, barely taking root,
>   when he blows on them and they wither.
> The wind carries them off like chaff.
> "To whom will you compare me?
>   Who is my equal?" asks the Holy One.

> Look up into the heavens.
> Who created all the stars?
> He brings them out like an army, one after another,
> calling each by its name.
> Because of his great power and incomparable strength,
> not a single one is missing.
> (Isaiah 40:21-26)

Do these verses help you gain a better picture of how far above us—in every way—is the Creator of the universe?

God Controls Everything

As humans, we sometimes think we have mastered our own lives. We go where we want to go, make our own schedules, live as we want to live. We have jobs and own houses and cars. We think not only that we are in control of our lives, but we also think we own what is ours.

But the Bible tells us otherwise. It shows us who is really in control, who really owns what we think is ours:

> "O LORD, the God of our ancestor Israel, may you be praised forever and ever! Yours, O LORD, is the greatness, the power, the glory, the victory, and the majesty. Everything in the heavens and on earth is yours, O LORD, and this is your kingdom. We adore you as the one who is over all things. Wealth and honor come from you alone, for you rule over everything. Power and might are in your hand, and at your discretion people are made great and given strength" (1 Chronicles 29:11-12).

Whenever we compare ourselves in our weaknesses with God's strength, we can see that there really is no comparison. This is God's universe, and He controls it all.

God Created the Universe with No Effort

What kind of picture do you have of God when He created the world? When we make something, we sweat and grunt and get tired.

But that's not true of God. His ability is so overpowering that creation was simple for Him. Psalm 33:6-9 describes how He created:

> The LORD merely spoke,
> and the heavens were created.
> He breathed the word,
> and all the stars were born.
> He assigned the sea its boundaries
> and locked the oceans in vast reservoirs.
> Let the whole world fear the LORD,
> and let everyone stand in awe of him.
> For when he spoke, the world began!
> It appeared at his command.

The power of God's words called the world into existence. His abilities as a Creator are beyond our imagination. But when we see His power and intelligence, it gives us confidence to trust Him with every detail of our lives.

The Work of the Trinity in Creation

Perhaps you have wondered, *Who actually created the universe? Was it God the Father?* The amazing answer to this question is that the Bible tells us that all three members of the triune God—the Father, the Son, and the Holy Spirit—participated in the creation. Look at Genesis 1:26 to understand this fact: "Then God said, 'Let *us* make human beings in *our* image, to be like *us*'" (emphasis added). Who is *us* and *our*? This is a reference to the Trinity. The Bible shows us that the Father, Son, and Holy Spirit agree and act as one. Let me offer further proof about the presence of all three persons of the Trinity at the creation:

God the Father—"By faith we understand that the entire universe was formed at God's command" (Hebrews 11:3). (Note: because this is a New Testament verse, the term *God* refers to the Father.)

Jesus—"God created everything through him, and nothing was created except through him" (John 1:3).

Holy Spirit—"His Spirit made the heavens beautiful" (Job 26:13).

This leads us to another question: What about God's character gives Him the ability to create and sustain the universe?

The Powerful Attributes of God

One of the key things we gain from reading and studying the Bible is a deepening understanding of who God is. We understand God by understanding His characteristics or attributes. Some of God's attributes are His alone: He is eternal, He is all-knowing. But some of His attributes can be reflected in our lives, such as the fact that He is love.

Although we can learn about many attributes of God throughout His Word, the ones listed below are characteristics that relate to the glory and power of His role as Creator.

God is infinite. If you stand at the seashore and look over the expanse of the ocean, you have probably caught a glimpse of what infinity must be. The water goes beyond the horizon, seemingly without end. Similarly, God has no limits, no boundaries, no beginning or end. That also means that all His other qualities—His love, mercy, and holiness—have no limits.

God is self-sufficient. If you walk out into Death Valley in the summer at high noon with no hat and no water, you'll shortly discover that you are not self-sufficient. You need external protection and help to avoid the life-threatening effects of dehydration and sunstroke. God, however, doesn't need anything—and He never has. He doesn't need help. And He doesn't need us. He depends on nothing outside Himself.

God is all-powerful. We get a taste of God's power in studying His work as Creator. To repeat parts of a verse I mentioned earlier: "We adore you as the one who is over all things...you rule over everything. Power and might are in your hand" (1 Chronicles 29:11-12). God's power is limitless. He says, "Everything I plan will come to pass, for I do whatever I wish" (Isaiah 46:10). In another verse God says,

> "From eternity to eternity I am God.
> No one can snatch anyone out of my hand.
> No one can undo what I have done."
> (Isaiah 43:13)

God's ability to do all things is called His omnipotence.

God is present everywhere. Time or space does not limit God. He is just as much with you as He is with me. King David writes of God,

> I can never escape from your Spirit!
>> I can never get away from your presence!
> If I go up to heaven, you are there;
>> if I go down to the grave, you are there.
>> (Psalm 139:7-8)

God says this of Himself: "Am I not everywhere in all the heavens and earth?" (Jeremiah 23:24). This means that God is present everywhere at the same time. We call this attribute God's omnipresence.

God knows everything. Think about that. God knows everything about everything. He knows the past, the present, and the future. In Isaiah we read,

> "Remember the things I have done in the past.
>> For I alone am God!
>> I am God, and there is none like me.
> Only I can tell you the future
>> before it even happens."
>> (Isaiah 46:9-10)

He knows *your* past, present, and future. He knows every thought you've ever had. God does not need to learn anything new, and nothing you do will surprise Him.

> The LORD looks down from heaven
>> and sees the whole human race.
> From his throne he observes
>> all who live on the earth.
> He made their hearts,
>> so he understands everything they do.
>> (Psalm 33:13-15)

So the God who sees the millions of eyeless shrimp miles under the ocean also sees what's in your heart. We call this attribute God's omniscience.

God is eternal. Time is a dimension that God created, and it does not bind Him. He lives outside of time. It baffles my mind to realize that God experiences all past, present, and future events simultaneously. He has no beginning and no end. Because God is eternal and because He has called us into relationship with Himself, He wants us to spend eternity with Him.

How do you respond to the Creator God after learning about His unlimited abilities and attributes? Are you afraid to approach Him? Do you believe that He is so far above you that He cannot relate to you? While He is the awesome Creator, He is also your Friend and Father. How should you respond? The psalmist urges us to respond to God with praise:

> O Lord, our Lord, your majestic name fills the earth!
>   Your glory is higher than the heavens.
> You have taught children and infants
>   to tell of your strength,
> silencing your enemies
>   and all who oppose you.
>   (Psalm 8:1-2)

> Shout joyful praises to God, all the earth!
>   Sing about the glory of his name!
>   Tell the world how glorious He is.
>   (Psalm 66:2)

> Yes, you have been with me from birth;
>   from my mother's womb you have cared for me.
> No wonder I am always praising You!
>   (Psalm 71:6)

Are you excited about God the Creator, the God who made and governs all things? He made not only the entire universe, but He also made *you*, with all of your uniqueness and complexity. He knows everything about you—and He loves you with a limitless love. Throughout the rest of this day, think about your Creator God, and praise Him for His greatness, His omnipotence, omnipresence, and omniscience.

God is not only the Creator, He is also the judge, who acts with utter integrity. The next chapter will explore those attributes.

DISCOVER THE TREASURE

Now that you are familiar with the observation process in Bible study, I would like you to move on to adding a map or plan to help you get more out of your study. The map involves four parts: *say, mean, apply,* and *fit.* Let me explain how each is designed to help you understand and apply the truths in the passage, and then I'll give you a passage you can practice the map with.

1. Ask: What does the passage *say*?

With this question, determine simple facts, such as who is speaking, the person(s) the passage is talking about, the general subject and subtopics, and the setting. Also look for basic information such as when the event occurred (historical and cultural background) and the characteristics of the main character(s).

2. Ask: What does the passage *mean*?

From the basic facts you can then find the meaning in the text. Identify the main principles and the lessons learned. To help you understand areas that are not clear to you in the passage, look up cross-references before you consult your study aids. Remember that the Bible is its own best commentary.

3. Ask: How can I *apply* the passage to my daily life?

Design an action plan to put the principles and lessons into practice. Then write out a personal prayer related to the main application, asking the Holy Spirit to help you apply it to your life.

4. Ask: How does the passage *fit* into or relate to the rest of Scripture?

No passage of Scripture stands alone. Each correlates with the whole theme of a chapter, book, and the entire Bible. Read other portions of Scripture related to the passage you are studying to see how they fit together. Also scan the entire book the passage is recorded in to get a clearer idea of how the passage relates to the whole.

Read Isaiah 40:21-31.

Work through each point in the map, recording your thoughts in your notebook. The third point, *apply*, will help you use the scriptural principles in your everyday life. Be sure to write down some specific ways you can do this. Also remember to record some prayer points.

1. What does the passage *say?*
2. What does the passage *mean?*
3. How can I *apply* the passage to my daily life?
4. How does the passage *fit* into or relate to the rest of Scripture?

Prayer Points:

10

Our Perfect Judge

id you follow the federal court's battle several years ago against the Alabama judge and his wish to display the Ten Commandments? The case set off a national furor with all the major media covering the ensuing public protest in front of the Alabama capitol building.

The man in the center of the storm was Judge Roy S. Moore, Alabama Supreme Court chief justice. When he ran for office, he pledged to restore the moral foundation of Alabama laws. After he was elected by an overwhelming margin, he installed a granite monument of the Ten Commandments in the rotunda of the capitol building. Judge Moore said, "In order to establish justice, we must invoke 'the favor and guidance of Almighty God.'"[7]

Predictably, three months later the American Civil Liberties Union, the Americans United for Separation of Church and State, and the Southern Poverty Law Center brought suit against Moore to have the granite monument removed in spite of tremendous support by the people of Alabama for Judge Moore's action. The organizations charged that the monument violated the First Amendment.

For two years the case wound its way through the court system, arriving at the bench of US District Judge Myron Thompson. He ruled that the monument must go.

Judge Moore refused to obey the district court's ruling. Four days before the deadline to remove the Ten Commandments, a rally was held in Montgomery to protest the monument's removal and to show support for Judge Moore's courage. Thousands of people came to cheer him on, including many national Christian leaders. Petitions urging the court to reverse its decision poured in from people around the country. In spite of this support, Judge Moore was suspended from his position as judge for his stance on the Ten Commandments.

Protestors began spending night and day in front of the capitol building, hoping to prevent the authorities from removing the monument. But in September 2003, workers rolled the monument out of the rotunda and into a room out of the public eye. The five-thousand-pound monument was gone, and the rotunda was empty.

What symbolic significance we can find in this tragic story. Undoubtedly, the Ten Commandments and other Scripture passages were the foundation for American law and the Constitution. The Bible is what made the American system of government the best in the world.

The Ten Commandments—and all of God's laws—are like that granite monument. They are unchangeable, written in the stone of God's standards. I know that God's laws are the only way that America will survive. Yet, Americans are turning their backs on the standards that make their country great and moral.

If the Ten Commandments are removed from public discourse, nothing can take their place. No other code, law, opinion, court decree, or trend can supplant the laws God has instigated for the whole world.

Why are these laws so important? Because they are an extension of God's attributes. He is holy, truthful, righteous, and just. Only He can set the standard. Only He can judge the world. In this chapter, we will see why God's nature makes Him the perfect judge.

The Law and the Judge

Several years ago, Scott, a senior in high school, began dating Melissa. He hadn't dated much, so he was thrilled when Melissa showed him a lot of attention. In fact, she seemed bent on becoming his girlfriend. *Wow,* Scott thought, *she picked me!*

But he had one problem. All his friends advised him against getting involved with her. They had heard rumors about her attitudes and actions at her last school. They said, "She's trouble. She's caused problems for every guy she's dated."

Scott ignored his friends. Melissa encouraged him to stay away from them and spend all his time with her.

When Scott's mother met Melissa, she was upset. "I'm sure she's not a Christian, Scott. And you know our rule about not dating someone who isn't a believer."

"She says she's a Christian, Mom. She even goes to church once in a while." But deep down, Scott knew that Melissa wasn't a believer and had no interest in spiritual things.

As the months flew by and Christmas vacation passed, the couple's relationship deteriorated. Melissa became very controlling—and Scott felt uncomfortable around her. But it was hard to reverse course and break off the relationship. Then one day they had a boisterous and hateful argument at her parents' house. Scott walked away from her—and the relationship.

Three days later, Scott was served with a notice that Melissa had filed a restraining order against him for domestic violence. This was terrible news. He was innocent, but how could he prove that he had never raised a hand against her? And a further fact terrified him. Graduation was coming up soon, and he had always dreamed of going into a law enforcement career. But that door would close if he was convicted of a violent act. His dreams would be smashed.

This was a time when Scott deeply felt his need for prayer. He and his parents brought the problem before God.

When the court date came, Scott found himself standing before a judge whose bench towered above him. Because Scott had turned eighteen just a month earlier, his parents were not allowed to be by his side. Alone, he had to face the power of the law and the judge.

Thoughts whirled through his mind. *What if the judge is unfair? Melissa has my future in her hands. What if there is some law that can be twisted in her favor?* He felt tongue-tied and helpless.

The case didn't take long. The judge heard Melissa's complaint and Scott's defense. Then she looked over the evidence, which mainly consisted of emails Scott had sent to Melissa. The courtroom became so quiet that it sounded like the inside of a tomb. Finally, the judge ruled.

"I've read the evidence and heard your stories. I find that there is no evidence of any violent actions in this case. Case dismissed." She pounded her gavel and set aside the paperwork.

Scott's knees felt weak. As he turned to leave the courtroom, he met his parents in the aisle. Their grins told it all.

This true story illustrates an important fact about any court system. Two components make the difference in the outcome—the law and the judge. If the law is unjust, the judge's ruling will by necessity be unjust. However, if the judge is unjust, he or she can twist the law to suit unfair purposes.

God's Law and God's Justice

Can you imagine what would happen in America if one Supreme Court justice enacted all the laws and oversaw their enforcement? Justice would reflect the heart of that judge—for good or for evil. Even in our American justice system, which attempts to balance power, we find unfairness and even evil. Think back over some of the Supreme Court rulings in the past decades. The most infamous is *Roe v. Wade,* which created a woman's "right" to an abortion. This has led to the deaths of millions of babies.

Unless a justice system has moral bedrock under it, it can never be fair or just. That's what makes the loss of the Ten Commandments in our government's arena so tragic.

The Ten Commandments reflect the heart of God. His attributes of integrity make Him both a perfect lawgiver and a perfect judge. He both controls the laws and metes out judgment. What are these attributes, and why do they make such a difference?

God's Qualities as a Judge

What makes a law good? What makes a judge fair? To get a clearer picture of God's role as a judge, we'll briefly examine four of His attributes: His *holiness, truthfulness, righteousness,* and *justice.* Each is indispensable to how God judges all things.

God's Holiness

This world is made up of contrasts. We can't understand the beauty of light unless we experience darkness. We can't appreciate peace unless we go through tumultuous times. We can't understand evil unless we recognize what is good. In a similar way, God's holiness reveals the nature of sin in this world. His holiness is the standard for all that is right and good.

But it's hard to get a handle on God's holiness because His perfection is so above us that our minds can't imagine it. He doesn't live up to a holy standard; He *is* the standard. Let me explain what this means through an analogy.

If you stand in a doorway and hold a mirror in sunlight to cast light into a dark room, you might say, "The mirror is lighting up the room." But that's not exactly true. The mirror is just bouncing sunlight off its surface. The light actually existed before it hit the mirror.

But if you open the drapes and let in the sunlight from outside the window, you could say, "The sun is lighting up the room." That would be true because the sun is a ball of light that shines its rays outward. The sun does not get its light from anywhere else.

God's holiness is His nature. He is holy through and through. He generates holiness; He did not acquire it.

In fact, the Bible tells us that holiness is a key characteristic in God's nature. When the Old Testament prophet Isaiah encountered God, he heard the angels around God's throne cry out,

> "Holy, holy, holy is the LORD Almighty;
> the whole earth is full of his glory."
> (Isaiah 6:3 NIV)

God's holiness is so perfect that it separates Him from everything else. Isaiah 40:25 says,

> "To whom will you compare me?
> Who is my equal?" asks the Holy One.

Once again, the prophet writes,

> The high and lofty one who lives in eternity,
>   the Holy One, says this:
> "I live in the high and holy place
>   with those whose spirits are contrite and humble."
>   (Isaiah 57:15)

We cannot reach up to touch God in His holiness. *The Praise and Worship Study Bible* says of God's holiness:

> God is the Holy One—set apart from all others. There is no one who can compare with him, for he is greater than all. Sometimes we lose sight of God's holiness, perhaps because we mistake his compassion and concern for us as equality with us. Although God does indeed care for us, he remains completely holy, and we should regard him with humility and reverence. Let us worship the Holy One, who has no equal.[8]

Can you see why God's holiness is so essential to His role as judge? Nothing in His nature comes between Him and His perfect standard. His holiness is what makes Him the perfect lawgiver.

Perhaps now you can also begin to grasp why God hates sin so much. It is the antithesis of His nature and the perversion of His laws. Just as a flyspeck in a glass of milk would make us shudder, God cannot tolerate sin of any kind. In the next chapter we will find out why God, who is perfect, can have anything to do with us humans, who are so full of sin.

God's Truth

Have you ever watched a piano tuner? The technician uses a tuning fork as he tightens the strings of a piano until they sound the correct pitch. The process, however, never works the other way around. The tuner never uses the piano strings to tune the tuning fork. That makes no sense and would not produce beautiful music.

God's truth is life's tuning fork. We set our thinking and actions to match His truth, not the other way around.

Have you noticed how the world tries to change truth to fit its opinions? That's like a piano tuner who changes the fork to match the piano's tones. The Bible says that sex outside of marriage is wrong. (That's the tuning-fork truth.) But people want to indulge in all kinds of sexual experiences, so they say, "It's okay to have sex outside of marriage as long as you love your partner." That's the piano trying to make the tuning fork change its pitch. But the tuning fork's pitch is absolute; it cannot change and still be a tuning fork. So it is with God's truth. His truth is absolute. That truth has never changed from eternity past, and it will never change in the future.

God's truth issues from His holiness. A holy God can never distort the truth by even a hair's breadth. Psalm 119:160 (NIV) assures us, "All your words are true; all your righteous laws are eternal." And Jesus said of Himself, "I am...the truth" (John 14:6).

When God says in the Ten Commandments, "You must not commit adultery," that truth is as valid today as it was when Moses received the tablets on Mount Sinai. We can shove aside God's laws, but His truth is still written in stone and unchangeable.

God's Righteousness

Have you ever wondered what the difference is between God's holiness and His righteousness? Let me explain it this way: Each person in the world grows up in a certain culture. That's true of an American, a Tibetan, or an Iraqi. Let's think about a man who is born into a Mexican home. His culture molds his personality. He will develop certain kinds of relationships with his family, will prefer specific kinds of foods, and will speak a particular language. He will see the world through Latin American eyes. We could say that he has a Latin American heart. His way of looking at the world causes him to act in certain ways. Perhaps he is friendlier to strangers than someone from urban New York might be.

Now let's apply this analogy to God's holiness and righteousness.

God's nature is holy. That is who He is. His holiness causes Him to act a certain way—righteously. Because God is holy, He is always truthful. Therefore, He cannot lie. His holiness causes Him to enforce the standard, "Do not lie."

A perfect judge must operate out of a holy nature with righteous pronouncements. As Scott realized, the judge who heard his case must be fair and just. That comes from the heart of the judge. At the same time, the judge must enforce the laws already on the books. The law must be righteous to be an effective tool in the hands of a good judge.

Because God is holy and righteous, we need never fear that He will mess up the case. The psalmist writes,

> Your righteousness, O God, reaches to the highest heavens.
> You have done such wonderful things.
> Who can compare with you, O God?
> (Psalm 71:19)

What He says is right, and we can rely on His Word. As Psalm 119:137-138 assures us,

> O LORD, you are righteous,
>   and your regulations are fair.
> Your laws are perfect
>   and completely trustworthy.

God's Justice

The Supreme Court ruled on *Roe v. Wade* in 1973. You may wonder what kinds of discussions were going on between the justices at that time. On what were they basing their opinions? What kind of logic or standards were they using? We may never know the intimate details of their deliberations.

But I just wonder what would have changed if Jesus Christ, in all His glory and in the company of thousands of angels singing "Holy, holy, holy," had filled the judges' chambers while they were deliberating that fateful decision. How would those judges—or any others—react if they had to explain their actions directly to God? You can imagine that all the cases they heard and all the decisions they made under those conditions would have a decidedly different tone.

But God's justice *is* present at every moment in history. No one will get by with doing anything wrong, and all will face God's judgment. It is a comfort to know that God will hold accountable people who have wronged us; His justice will prevail. It is also a comfort to remember the good news that people who confess their sin and look to the death of Jesus Christ for forgiveness of that sin will receive full pardon for their wrongs.

What will it feel like to stand before a holy judge to receive justice? That will be an awesome and terrifying moment. And yet we can trust God because His justice is pure and holy. Because of His perfect integrity and sinlessness, He has all authority and power to judge.

God hates sin and loves justice. "I, the LORD, love justice. I hate...wrongdoing" (Isaiah 61:8). But He is also patient, desiring that all people recognize their sin, repent, find forgiveness in the sacrificial death of His Son, and so escape the judgment of eternal death.

When I think of God's justice, I want to tell everyone of His fairness. Deuteronomy 32:3-4 says,

> "I will proclaim the name of the LORD;
>   how glorious is our God!
> He is the Rock; his deeds are perfect.
>   Everything he does is just and fair.
> He is a faithful God who does no wrong;
>   how just and upright he is!"

We have an amazing God. Another facet of His nature is expressed in the Bible's most endearing and intimate picture of God—He is our gracious Savior. He loves us and wants to be in a relationship with us. In the next chapter we will see how magnificent our God is in His love for us.

But before you go on, take time to discover the awesome wonder of God's role as judge. The Discover the Treasure material will take you through a topical study on God as judge.

DISCOVER THE TREASURE

In the remaining chapters in this book, I will introduce you to three additional Bible-study methods—topical study, chapter or book study, and biographical study. You have already been using a smaller-scale method of a chapter study when you studied a portion of Scripture in the last few chapters.

In this study, you will use your map (*say, mean, apply, fit*) with a topical method of study. Think of your study in this way. The "say, mean, apply, fit" will show you where to go, like a map you take on a trip. The topical method of study is the vehicle used to get you to your destination, like taking a car on your trip. The Bible-study map gives the direction; the Bible-study method takes you to the place in the Bible you want to study.

For your topical study, you will need a Bible concordance, which is an alphabetical list of key words and where they're found in the Bible. You can find a concordance in the back of many Bibles or as part of most Bible software programs.

Because this chapter is about God our judge, for this exercise we will study the word *judge*. Look up the word in your concordance. The listing will give you the verses that contain the word *judge* as well as the words immediately surrounding it so that you can understand a bit of the context. In the New Living Translation, for example, the word *judge* appears 221 times. Obviously you will not want to do a study of all 221 passages, so read through the contextual words to find a few passages that speak specifically about God as our judge. I've inserted seven possible passages here and emphasized the word *judge* in each one. Choose three verses to study for this exercise.

- Genesis 18:25—Should not the *Judge* of all the earth do what is right?
- Psalm 7:11—God is an honest *judge*.
- Psalm 50:6—Then let the heavens proclaim his justice, for God himself will be the *judge*.

- Isaiah 33:22—For the LORD is our *judge*, our lawgiver, and our king. He will care for us and save us.

- Matthew 16:27—For the Son of Man will come with his angels in the glory of his Father and will *judge* all people according to their deeds.

- 2 Timothy 4:8—And now the prize awaits me—the crown of righteousness, which the Lord, the righteous *Judge*, will give me on the day of his return. And the prize is not just for me but for all who eagerly look forward to his appearing.

- Revelation 14:7—"Fear God," he shouted. "Give glory to him. For the time has come when he will sit as *judge*. Worship him who made the heavens, the earth, the sea, and all the springs of water."

Find the verses in context in your Bible and read all three passages. Then use the "say, mean, apply, fit" map to explore the passages. We'll go through one passage as an example:

Read Psalm 7.

1. What does the passage *say?*

The psalmist David is the speaker, and he is making an impassioned plea to God. Apparently David is being persecuted, and he looks to God for protection and judgment. The passage says that God—who looks deep within the mind and heart—is a judge who is perfectly honest (v. 11), who is righteous (v. 9), who is a shield saving those who are true and right (v. 10). David is trusting God to judge not only his persecutors but also himself (vv. 3-5).

2. What does the passage *mean?*

The passage means that the psalmist is awed and comforted by the fact that God is a just judge. He can count on God to vindicate him and protect him from his enemies. David can also trust God to judge him fairly.

3. How can I *apply* the passage to my daily life?

God is the judge in our lives too. We can count on Him to judge us fairly, to point out ways that we have not been true or fair. But we can also take comfort that God will judge people who have treated us unfairly, maybe a neighbor or coworker who has spread a rumor about us or maybe a parent who wronged us when we were young. God will judge them too, so we can rest, trusting His justice.

4. How does the passage *fit* into or relate to the rest of the Scripture?

This passage harmonizes not only with other psalms in which the psalmist cries out for God to judge evildoers but also with other passages that declare God the fair judge of nations and individuals (see other passages in the bulleted list above).

Before writing out prayer points, do a study of your three passages, writing out what you hear the passages say and mean, and how you feel they apply and fit. Then compare what you learned in the three passages. One of the advantages of this kind of topical study is that you arrive at a deeper and fuller understanding of the topic. Remember, you can do the topical study with many words, phrases, and topics, enriching your study of the Bible's teachings.

Prayer Points:

11

Our Loving Savior

Henrietta Mears was one of the most unusual women of her time. She served as the Christian education director at the Hollywood Presbyterian Church when I was a young man. Her influence was amazing. And she was instrumental in leading me to the truth about Jesus Christ.

One day as I listened to her teach from the Bible, I became deeply aware of her wisdom and boldness. She spoke with authority, yet I saw her genuine love for each of the young men and women in the audience. She taught that day about the apostle Paul's conversion from Judaism to Christianity, how Paul (whose name was Saul before it was changed to Paul) was traveling to Damascus to find more Christians to put to death. As he rode along, something amazing happened to him.

> "As I was on the road, approaching Damascus about noon, a very bright light from heaven suddenly shone down around me. I fell to the ground and heard a voice saying to me, 'Saul, Saul, why are you persecuting me?'
>
> "'Who are you, lord?' I asked.
>
> "And the voice replied, 'I am Jesus the Nazarene, the one you are persecuting.' The people with me saw the light but didn't understand the voice speaking to me.
>
> "I asked, 'What should I do, Lord?'" (Acts 22:6-10).

"'What should I do, Lord?' is one of the most important questions you can possibly ask of God, even today," Dr. Mears told us. "The happiest people in the world are those who are in the center of God's will. The most miserable are those who are not doing God's will. Paul deceived himself into thinking he was doing God's will by persecuting the Christians. In reality, he was pursuing his own ambitions. So God set him straight with the dramatic experience on the road to Damascus."

Then Dr. Mears said something that really hit home for me. "Now, not many of us have dramatic, emotional conversion experiences as Paul did. But the circumstances don't really matter. What matters is your response to the same questions: 'Who are you, Lord, and what do you want me to do?'" She challenged each of us to go home, get on our knees, and ask God those all-important questions.

As I returned to my apartment that night, I realized that I was ready to give my life to God. What attracted me to Dr. Mears's message and the gospel was God's love, which I had discovered through my study of the Bible and through the love of the people I had met at Hollywood Presbyterian Church.

I knelt beside my bed that night and asked the questions Dr. Mears had given us: "Who are you, Lord, and what do you want me to do?" In a sense, that was my prayer for salvation. It wasn't theologically profound, but the Lord knew my heart, and He interpreted what was going on inside me.

Although nothing dramatic happened when I prayed, I know without a doubt that Jesus came into my life. I accepted Him, and He accepted me. I began to learn what true love was as I developed my relationship with God. That love has sustained me over these years. Today I understand even more deeply the love God has given me.

So far, we have learned that the Bible presents God as a powerful Creator and a perfect judge. But the most endearing picture of God is that of a gracious Savior. Through Jesus Christ and His birth, life, death, and resurrection we clearly see the attributes of God's relationship to us.

Our Relationship with God

The attributes that describe God's relationship to us reveal His heart and desire to redeem us. His love provides the plan to redeem us. His mercy brought Jesus to sacrifice Himself for us. His faithfulness took Jesus through all the pain and sorrow to accomplish the goal set before Him. His unchanging nature (immutability) made it possible for God to plan for our redemption before time began.

Let's look at what the Bible says about each of these attributes.

God Is Love

One day I was reading the prayer of Jesus found in John 17. This was the prayer He offered just before He submitted Himself to death on the cross. I came to verses 22 and 23: "I have given them the glory you gave me, so they may be one as we are one. I am in them and you are in me. May they experience such perfect unity that the world will know that you sent me and that you love them as much as you love me." I leaped out of my chair in amazement. I realized that God promises to love us as much as He loves His one and only Son. What is more, He loves us unconditionally and supernaturally. He loves us simply because He is a God of love, not because we are good or worthy.

God's love is described in 1 Corinthians 13:

> Love is patient and kind. Love is not jealous or boastful or proud or rude. It does not demand its own way. It is not irritable, and it keeps no record of being wronged. It does not rejoice about injustice but rejoices whenever the truth wins out. Love never gives up, never loses faith, is always hopeful, and endures through every circumstance (vv. 4-7).

Doesn't it give you a feeling of incredible comfort to know that God loves you in this way? God's love is perfect; it has no flaws, no end to its depth. It is unconditional. Nothing we can do or say will change God's love for us.

God is the source of all love. It is the supreme expression of His nature. The Bible tells us that God *is* love (1 John 4:8). The Old

Testament says, "The LORD is good. His unfailing love continues forever" (Psalm 100:5). That is a reassuring truth.

God's greatest love was shown through sacrifice. Have you ever heard the saying, "Something's not worth anything until you have to sacrifice something for it"? God proved how much we are worth to Him by sacrificing Jesus Christ to die a horrible death on a cross and to take upon Himself the sins of the world. The suffering of the physical pain on the cross was nothing compared to the agony of Christ, the sinless one, taking on the sins of the world. We cannot imagine the sacrifice Jesus made to do this for us.

God's love is based in His goodness. His goodness is evident in universal blessings such as the sunshine and rainfall and all the necessities of life He provides. But His goodness is also shown in the affection He displays. Psalm 145:9 says, "The LORD is good to everyone. He showers compassion on all his creation."

Have you ever received a blessing that you just didn't feel entitled to? That's God's goodness.

I remember one particular time when God's goodness seemed so real to me. Vonette and I were flying from New York to Washington, DC, during a frightful storm. Lightning flashed as the aircraft bounced and shuddered in the turbulence.

Then a calm voice came over the intercom, "Ladies and gentlemen, we should be out of the storm in a few minutes." The words seemed hollow as a fresh blast of the storm rattled the plane.

I gripped Vonette's hand and said, "I don't know how much longer the plane can endure this storm without breaking into pieces."

The 707 began to twist—first to the right and then to the left. Its wings flapped like those of a great bird struggling against a violent downdraft. Vonette and I began praying. Convinced that our aircraft couldn't survive the turbulence much longer, I tenderly said good-bye to Vonette and she to me. We told our wonderful Lord that we were ready to meet Him.

Then I remembered how the Lord Jesus had calmed the winds when His disciples feared that their boat would capsize during another violent storm. If it was God's will, He could protect us too. I prayed aloud, "Lord, You control the laws of nature. You quieted the storm on the Sea of Galilee. Please quiet this storm."

In a very short time, the rain and the turbulence stopped. Amazed and thankful, Vonette and I praised God for protecting us.

Hours later, the pilot landed the plane at a flight terminal in Norfolk, Virginia. The flight that should have taken a little over an hour had lasted four hours and had taken us far from our destination. Lightning had knocked a huge hole in the fuselage near the cockpit, destroying all the radar equipment. The pilot said this was the most violent storm he had ever experienced. But God was more powerful than the storm. Our survival was an act of His goodness and love.

God Is Merciful

If you think about the situation after Creation, God really had a dilemma. The people He created and loved rebelled against Him. They sinned, and their sin filled the earth. Because God is perfectly holy, He could not wink at sin; He had to punish it. Because God is just, His punishment was not just a slap on the wrist. The consequence of humanity's sin was eternal separation from God. But because God is merciful, He was pained to see His creatures suffer eternal separation. What could He do?

Of course, God never felt confused or unable to plan the future. He had a plan before time began. He knew mankind would sin, and He knew how He would respond. God, in His infinite mercy, could love His creation and at the same time be perfectly holy and just. And He would do that through Jesus Christ's sacrifice as Savior of the world. Through Christ's death for us on the cross

- God's holiness was satisfied since our sins were blotted out.
- God's justice was meted out because our sins were fully paid.
- God's mercy was fulfilled because He could open His arms to those who were cleansed.

Ephesians 2:4-5 says, "God is so rich in mercy, and he loved us so much, that even though we were dead because of our sins, he gave us life when he raised Christ from the dead." And God's mercy is what brings us peace.

One day I visited a high-security men's penitentiary filled with murderers, drug dealers, rapists, bank robbers, and others who had committed violent crimes. Many of the prisoners I met would never again walk outside those bleak, gray prison walls. At an evangelistic service, however, one inmate after another stood to share how, even though he had committed a serious crime, he knew that he was a child of God.

Many of these men expressed their joy in this way: "I'm so glad that I'm in prison because I found Jesus Christ as my Savior and Lord here. I would rather be in prison with Christ in my heart than live in a mansion without any knowledge of God's love and forgiveness."

I thought about how true their words were. I have met many wealthy and educated men and women who have no peace. Having fame, possessions, money, friends, or freedom cannot guarantee peace. Only God's mercy gives us true peace.

God Is Faithful

I can think of no story in the Old Testament that better illustrates God's faithfulness than the story of Joseph. He was sold into slavery by his brothers and taken to Egypt, far from home. A man named Potiphar purchased Joseph and eventually put Joseph in charge of his entire household. Joseph, true to his God, worked hard and honestly to serve his master. But then Potiphar's wife accused Joseph of sexual advances, and Potiphar threw Joseph into prison. There Joseph, an innocent man, was seemingly forgotten for years. It seemed that God had neglected one of His own.

But in a miraculous turn of events through the revelation of a dream to Joseph, he was elevated to work in the court of Pharaoh, the most powerful man in the kingdom. Joseph served his new master well, and Pharaoh gave over much of the realm's responsibility to Joseph.

God had been with Joseph throughout the tough years. Now God was ready to use Joseph to save a budding nation—Israel. God revealed to Joseph that a great famine was coming and that he should prepare

Egypt. Joseph listened to God and put aside a large portion of the country's harvest for the next seven years. When the famine came, the people had plenty to eat and even some to sell to the nations around them.

Joseph's brothers eventually came to Egypt to buy food, and unbeknownst to them, it was Joseph—the brother they had sold into slavery—who mercifully preserved their lives by providing food for them when the famine came. Joseph met with his brothers and revealed his identity to them. When his brothers learned who he was, they were afraid of retribution. But Joseph said to them, "You intended to harm me, but God intended it for good to accomplish what is now being done, the saving of many lives" (Genesis 50:20 NIV). This story is a picture of God's faithfulness—to Joseph and to his family.

Has a friend or family member ever betrayed you? Perhaps your betrayal wasn't as serious as Joseph's, but remember the truth of the story: God will not turn His back on you. His faithfulness means that He will always be by your side. First Corinthians 1:9 says, "God is faithful, who has called you into fellowship with his Son, Jesus Christ our Lord" (NIV). He is faithful through difficult circumstances and in protecting us from temptation. He is even faithful to us when we are unfaithful to Him. God's faithfulness means

- He always keeps His promises.
- He will always love us.
- His mercy is unending toward those who love Him.

God Never Changes

Considering God's faithfulness inevitably leads us to the fact that He never changes. In fact, He is the only being who stays the same. This is called God's immutability.

This attribute of God means that He never grows or develops. That's because He is perfect and knows all things, so His wisdom is always complete. He never has to learn anything either. And He never has to perfect any part of His nature.

This concept is so far out of our experience that we have a hard time grasping it. But God's immutability should give us complete confidence in placing our lives in His hands.

That's also why I have so much trust in God's Word. It reflects the immutability of God.

In 1982, I had the privilege of serving as chairman of a national congress on the Bible held in San Diego, California. Thousands of Christian leaders came from across the country and from other countries. More than fifty leading scholars addressed the various plenary and seminar sessions. We met to affirm our confidence in the Word of God as holy, inspired, and without error. We all related ways that the unchanging nature of God's Word is the foundation of our lives.

At Campus Crusade, we are dedicated to reaching the world with the gospel. We have used many methods of spreading the message: one-on-one evangelism, major conferences, concerts, magic shows, and various types of publications. We try to be as creative as possible in reaching the hearts of unbelievers. But our message never changes. It is the eternal story of God's love, mercy, and faithfulness.

Resting in God

What benefit do we receive because of God's love, mercy, faithfulness, and immutability? We can rest in Him—no matter what happens. When things look the worst, God is still in charge—and He never fails.

This is illustrated so wonderfully by the experience of Joni Eareckson Tada, who was paralyzed from the neck down in a diving accident when she was only nineteen years old. She went through a period of wrenching depression. This is how she describes her pain:

> I remember the dark days, when I would shut myself in a dark bedroom. Days when I was still in the hospital, and at nighttime, when it would get so lonely, I would sing hymns like "Savior, Thou art calling, do not pass me by." I would sing that line face up on a Stryker frame at night.

When they would flip me face down to keep me from getting bedsores, I would have a pencil in my mouth to flip the pages of the Bible. After having sung that hymn one night, "Pass Me Not, O Gentle Savior," I turned to a favorite portion of Scripture [John 5], and it became my prayer.[9]

At that time, Joni couldn't imagine what God had in store for her. She wanted so much to be completely healed, but that was not God's plan for her life. Over the years, God's good plan began to work itself out. But back in the early days of her debilitation, she didn't know about the ministry, Joni and Friends, that the Lord would lead her to establish. She couldn't see the encouragement and growth she would inspire in other handicapped people. She didn't recognize the personal growth that her limitations would help her produce in the Spirit.

Once she got out of the hospital during those trial years, God began to produce peace and patience in her life. Today, she says to the Lord,

"I am so glad that You did not pass me by, because a 'no' answer to my urgent request for healing has meant strengthened commitment, a refined character. I have eschewed evil and cleave to that which is good. It has meant a more buoyant, happy hope of heaven. It has meant a more deepened prayer life and sensitivity to others who are disabled. Oh, Lord God, thank You, thank You."[10]

Joni spoke these words at our 2001 Campus Crusade for Christ staff conference. Knowing Joni and seeing her spirit, no one could doubt that she is resting her soul in our loving, unchanging God.

That can be your experience too. When we immerse ourselves in the Bible, we also will see miraculous changes in our hearts as we learn about God's nature and allow His Spirit to mold us into Christ's image.

So, these are the attributes we covered:

God Our Creator

- God's limitlessness (He is infinite and eternal)
- God's self-sufficiency

- God's omnipotence
- God's omnipresence
- God's omniscience

God Our Judge

- God's holiness
- God's truthfulness
- God's righteousness
- God's justice

God Our Savior

- God's love
- God's mercy
- God's faithfulness
- God's immutability

This is a magnificent and glorious list. In the next chapter we will ask this question: How do we respond to God's nature?

DISCOVER THE TREASURE

Once again, we will be using the "say, mean, apply, fit" method of Bible study. This time, however, choose a topic that will help you with a challenge you are facing right now. You might want to choose one of the following topics:

- Worry
- Fear
- Giving

- Temptation
- Hope
- Doubt
- Comfort
- Protection

Remember the steps we outlined in the last chapter:

1. Look up the word in a concordance.

2. From the list of verses given, evaluate the word in its context and select the verses you want to study in greater depth.

3. Find the verses in your Bible and read the surrounding passages.

4. Answer the following questions for each passage.

1. What does the passage *say?*

With this question, determine simple facts such as who is speaking, what people the passage might be talking about, the general subject, and the setting. Also, look for basic information, such as when the event occurred (historical and cultural background) and the characteristics of the main character(s).

2. What does the passage *mean?*

From the basic facts, you can then find the meaning in the text. Identify the main principles and the lessons learned. To help you understand areas that are not clear to you in the passage, look up cross-references before you consult your study aids. Remember that the Bible is its own best commentary.

3. How can I *apply* the passage to my daily life?

Design an action plan to put the principles and lessons into practice. Then write out a personal prayer related to the main application, asking the Holy Spirit to help you apply it to your life.

4. How does the passage *fit* into or relate to the rest of Scripture?

No passage of Scripture stands alone. Each correlates with the whole theme of a chapter, book, and the entire Bible. Scan the entire book (look at the passage headings) in which the passage is recorded to get a clearer idea of how the passage relates to the whole. Compare what the various passages say about the same topic.

Prayer Points:

12

Responding to God

In the 1920s, missionaries came to the Ethiopian highlands to tell the people about God's love and forgiveness. When they visited Mahay Choramo's town, Soddo, he turned away from his pagan religion and followed Jesus. He was just a child at the time.

Right away, Mahay began learning how to read the Amharic language well enough so that he could study the Bible. Eventually, he translated portions of the Bible for the people living around Soddo.

As the truths of the Bible began to work deeply in Mahay's heart, what he learned inspired him to minister to others. He began helping the poor. He kept his witness for his Lord strong and vibrant. During times of government persecution of Christians during the 1940s and 1950s, he went before the government officials with his Bible in his hand, using it as his defense. He told others about Jesus Christ.

Decade after decade, Mahay worked in southwest Ethiopia, including Banna territory, the home of warring tribes, where Mahay lived with the people, becoming friends with the ones he hoped to reach. He endured much hardship, including the murder of a colleague who had come to live with him and minister to the Banna people.

Today, at eighty-one years of age, Mahay still earns less than forty dollars per month, but he has not tired of seeing people find peace in Christ. One of the missionaries who works with Mahay, Doug Stinson, described him as "an eighty-one-year-old evangelist [who] sports a baseball cap and several days' stubble of beard. His shoulders are slumped, and one hand rests on the dashboard. He dozes as we travel the rough road. He's going to fetch a blind boy to enroll him in the School for the Blind in Wolaitta, Mahay's home area. He says he would have walked the two-day journey to get the boy if I hadn't been going."[11] Mahay is an example of someone who began to study the Bible and responded to God's love by letting what he learned transform him into an ambassador for Christ.

The Bible is God's voice to us. How responsive are you to what you are hearing? How does God feel about your response to Him? Are you doing all the talking, making your conversation a one-way street? Is your mind traveling so fast that you don't have time to listen to His voice? God speaks in truth and wisdom, but are you tuned in to His frequency?

Through our study of the Bible so far, we have learned many awesome truths about God's character, but they aren't merely facts to file away. God wants us to respond to Him. He has taken the first step in the dialogue through giving us His Word. Now it is our turn to take what we learn and apply it to our lives and ministry.

Response and Communication

I once met a gangster who turned his life over to Christ. But in his spiritual immaturity, he kept some of his old ways. In an effort to befriend and disciple him, I gave him a *One Year Bible*, which guides a person through the Bible in a year, and it intoxicated this man. He just couldn't put the Bible down. He would read two or three days' selections—sometimes even a week's—in advance. Before he became a Christian, this man was spiritually illiterate. In fact, he had never read the Bible. But as he dug into the Word, his life was transformed. God reached out to save him from his sin, and he responded by spending time in God's Word and acknowledging by his actions what he read.

Bible reading and Bible study will change our lives as we listen intently to what God says and apply what we learn. Therefore, our first response should be to dig into the Bible, because that is how we get to know God better.

Next, we take what we learn in the Bible and use it to conform our lives to what we know about God through His Word. Let's look at other responses that Bible study can bring into our lives. The following list is not complete, of course, but practice the ones that seem appropriate for your life at the moment.

Responding to Our Creator

One of the foremost and crucial responses to the creator God is to praise Him. Praise takes the focus off us and places it on God, where it belongs. We can praise God in many ways. Some people like to have a quiet time in their backyard or in a park where they can enjoy nature and praise God for all they see, hear, and smell. The gentle crooning of a mourning dove or the soothing aroma of roses or of green grass makes it easy to praise our wonderful Creator. Other times we may want to praise God through song. Singing a praise chorus or a hymn of praise can set our hearts right toward God even before we begin reading His Word. Praying through psalms of praise is another way to praise God. If you want to practice this response, try using any of the following psalms as a prayer to God: Psalm 8, 19, 33, 47, 66, 92, 95, 104, 113, 135, or 146.

We can also respond to God's attributes as Creator.

- Because God is *infinite*, we can respond with hope. If you are enduring a difficult crisis right now, look at it in the light of God's limitless resources and ability. That will help you have a healthy perspective of your problem. Also, let God's infinite nature help you appreciate your connection with Him. Take a walk and look into the skies or at a mountain crest and thank Him for how magnificent He is. Tell Him how His relationship with you means so much to you.

- Because God is *self-sufficient*, we can respond with confidence in that whatever we ask of Him, He is able to do. He can provide for our needs—food, shelter, love from friends and family.

- Because God is *all-powerful*, we can claim His power to face difficult circumstances. When problems in your job or in a family relationship make you discouraged, remember that

God has the power to overcome any obstacle. Rely on God's power rather than your own self-will when you face trials.

- Because God is *present everywhere*, we can respond by practicing His presence, by talking to Him in silent prayer during many moments of the day, especially during times of duress or fear. Remember that He is right by your side and knows your situation and your every need. He is waiting to assist you in every way.

- Because God is *all-knowing*, we can respond with trust. When we place our lives in His hands, we can have confidence that He knows every detail of our lives—our thoughts, our motives, our desires. Nothing surprises Him. Do you have a sin that you are having difficulty handling? God knows about it. Turn it over to Him, and ask His forgiveness; then go on with confidence that He will not hold it against you.

- Because God is *eternal,* we can respond with awe. The God we serve has no beginning or end. This great, majestic God loves us enough to become involved in our everyday lives.

Do you see how practical our responses should be? They should be grounded in God's Word, then intertwined into the fabric of our lives. We should ask God to reveal ways we can confirm His work in our lives through how we speak, act, and worship.

Responding to Our Judge

Many people see God as an indulgent grandfather who pats them on the head when they do wrong and says, "There, there, you'll do better next time." But that portrait of God doesn't fit what we learned about God's attributes of integrity. One day God will judge the world—every person who has ever lived. No one will escape. God will judge those who have rejected His Son, Jesus Christ, and they will face the penalty of their sin. Believers will stand before God the judge, and their deeds, for good or for evil, will be revealed. Jesus will reward them for how they have lived for Him.

This reality of impending judgment should build in us a fear of God. For believers, this fear is not one of terror but a deep respect for our holy judge.

How do we respond to God, our perfect judge?

- God's *holiness* causes us to turn away from sin to live holy lives and to warn others of impending judgment. When we have a sense of God's holiness and His hatred for sin, we will want to live spotless lives in His power. And because we understand God's holy nature, we will warn people who don't know God to turn from their sin and accept God's forgiveness through Christ.

- We trust God and His Word completely because He is *truth*. In all things, we live by the truth in God's Word. When we are confused, God's Word helps us. When we need to judge our actions, God's Word is our standard.

- Understanding God's *righteousness* means that we live by His standards. Therefore, we study His Word to find His rules and principles to understand how they apply to our lives. Then we obey God's laws out of respect.

- We fight against injustice in the world because God is *just*. We help the poor and needy, the helpless and the sick. Our own cause is forgotten as we hold out our hands to others as Jesus held out His hands to the multitudes.

Our lives will never be perfect, but through the power of the Holy Spirit we must work toward living lives of integrity. When we reflect God's holiness, truth, righteousness, and justice, we help the world to see that His ways are different from their ways.

Responding to Our Savior

God's relationship attributes enable us to communicate intimately with Him. The creator of the universe has come to live with you and me, and the judge has paid the price for our sentence with His own life. What an awesome reality. How will you respond?

One of the most important ways we respond to God our Savior is by obeying Christ's command to partake of the Lord's Supper (1 Corinthians 11:23-32). This simple ceremony reminds us of the costly sacrifice Jesus made for us. This solemn time also helps us to reevaluate our spiritual direction and to focus our attention on our beloved Lord. I encourage you to join regularly in the communion around the Lord's Supper in the church that you attend.

But we can respond in other ways to Jesus Christ as our Savior and Lord.

- God is *love,* and an appropriate response to this love is to love others through our actions and our witness. When we respond self-sacrificially, when we give ourselves for the sake of another, we reflect our Savior's love and draw others to Him.

- We can respond to our Savior's *mercy* to us by showing mercy to others. What a tragedy if we who have been forgiven so much refuse to forgive someone who has wronged us. As we extend kindness and love, we reflect our Savior's mercy.

- We can respond to God's *faithfulness* by living lives marked by trustworthiness and patience. When we stick by someone through tough times, we reflect our Savior's faithfulness. When we patiently parent our children through the good and bad times, we honor Christ. When we keep our promises at home and at work, we mirror Christ's faithful love.

- We can respond to God's *unchanging nature* by resolving to live lives of integrity and stability. We can count on God to be the same yesterday, today, and tomorrow. Can our friends and family count on us for the same? Can they count on us to remain true to our word? Can they count on us to remain true to our commitment to Christ? When we hold to the truth, we reflect God's unchanging nature.

Are you ready to respond to God's character? Where do you think God is leading you right now in your study of God's Word? Has your study resulted in the kind of responses given above? The goal of Bible study is first to know God, then to allow God's Word to direct your life.

In the next section—Part 4: How Does the Bible Change My Life?—we will use our response to God as our starting point as we discover how the Bible can change our lives. Each of us can live above our circumstances in joy and peace as we apply what we have learned about God and His book so far.

DISCOVER THE TREASURE

Now that you have practiced studying several topics in your Bible study, we can move on to trying a different method of Bible study—a chapter study.

One of the greatest biblical passages about the Word of God is Psalm 119. Since the psalm has 176 verses, I suggest breaking up the study into several sessions. The Bible naturally breaks the psalm into sections, so use that for your selection process. Once again, use the "say, mean, apply, fit" map.

1. What does the passage *say*?

With this question, determine simple facts such as who is speaking in the passage, to whom he is speaking, what people the passage is talking about, the general subject, and the setting. What is troubling the writer, and what does he ask of God?

2. What does the passage *mean*?

From the basic facts, you can then find the meaning in the text. Identify the main principles and the lessons learned. What many things do you learn about the Bible from these verses? What is the psalmist learning about himself and his life? How is God's Word and God's nature significant to him?

3. How can I *apply* the passage to my daily life?

How does what the psalmist is learning apply to your life? Are his insights relevant? Are his declarations ones you can make? Design an action plan to put the principles and lessons into practice. Then write out a personal prayer related to the main application, asking the Holy Spirit to help you apply it to your life.

4. How does the passage *fit* into or relate to the rest of Scripture?

How does what you learned about the Bible in this chapter compare to other things you've learned about the Bible? How does this psalm fit with the other psalms?

Prayer Points:

PART 4

How Does the Bible Change My Life?

"We live in a world literally dying for Christians to be who the Bible says they are. Isn't it time we separated ourselves for God's purposes; isn't it time we become the people of God?"

BILL McCARTNEY

13

How Does the Bible Strengthen My Faith?

Throughout this book we have learned about the trustworthiness of the Bible, how we can understand its truths, and how it reveals the character of God to us. But our experience with the Bible must be more than merely learning. We must also allow God's Word to radically change us.

I am always encouraged to hear stories of how the Bible has touched people's lives. Often the stories are of people who were changed when they studied the Bible in a group or Sunday school class. They had the benefit of other wise believers and study aids. But what about people who have none of those things? Listen to the incredible story of a man whose life was changed by a most unusual encounter with the Word of God.

Because Hien Pham knew English, he was a translator for American soldiers during the Vietnam War. But when Vietnam fell, he was accused of being a spy for the Americans and was sent to a "re-education camp," where he was forced to clean latrines. His life was very restricted in the camp, and reading English books was forbidden. One day as Hien Pham was working in a latrine, he saw a printed page that someone had used as toilet paper. Recognizing English words, he washed off the paper and discovered it was a page from the Bible:

> And we know that in all things God works for the good
> of those who love him, who have been called according to

his purpose. For those God foreknew he also predestined to be conformed to the image of his Son, that he might be the firstborn among many brothers and sisters. And those he predestined, he also called; those he called, he also justified; those he justified, he also glorified.

What, then, shall we say in response to these things? If God is for us, who can be against us? He who did not spare his own Son, but gave him up for us all—how will he not also, along with him, graciously give us all things?...For I am convinced that neither death nor life, neither angels nor demons, neither the present nor the future, nor any powers, neither height nor depth, nor anything else in all creation, will be able to separate us from the love of God that is in Christ Jesus our Lord (Romans 8:28-32,38-39 NIV).

Hien Pham was overwhelmed by the powerful words of God, which comforted him and assured him that God loved him and had a plan for his life. If God could encourage him by using "toilet paper" in a filthy latrine in a communist prison camp, then God could certainly guide and protect his life. Nothing—not even brutal prison guards—could separate him from the love of God that is in Christ Jesus.[1]

The same God who touched Hien Pham's life can change your life through His Word. And God will change your life in two significant ways: by helping you develop a biblical worldview and by teaching you how to grow personally and spiritually.

The Bible Shapes Our Worldview

If someone asked you, "What is your worldview?" what would you answer? A worldview is any ideology or philosophy that shapes the way a person relates to his or her world. I'm sure you've encountered many different worldviews without specifically recognizing them as such. What ideas and beliefs motivate rock stars? What they think about eternal questions will affect the music people listen to on their way home from work. How does the worldview of a gay politician affect what he does? How does the grid through which he sees life change the lives of others? The worldview of an astrophysicist may be more complicated than that of a cattle rancher, but both have an interpretive framework through which they make sense of the world.

What about Christians? Do we have a worldview? Definitely. When we build our lives on the foundation of the Word of God, we live out of a biblical worldview. In his book *Earth Restored,* my friend John Barber defines how a Christian sees the world: "A biblical worldview is seeing the world as God sees it. It is thinking God's thoughts after Him in *all* areas of life. While many people think that God's Word only applies to areas like prayer, personal evangelism, and inward holiness, a biblical worldview assumes that the Bible also speaks to education, art, business, politics, technology, and more."[2]

How do we express a Christian worldview? Matt, an educator, asked a similar question in his Bible-study group. "I know what I'm expected to do in church and when I'm around my Christian friends. But what about when I'm at work? I feel that religion is a private matter and that it's not appropriate for me to share the Bible's perspective about things I discuss with my coworkers."

The other members of his group faced similar situations. Michelle, a neonatal nurse, was reluctant to talk to her colleagues about anything related to the Bible. Chad, a screenwriter, worked with a staff that regularly ridiculed anything remotely biblical or Christian. José, a graduate-school student in molecular biology, feared that if he mentioned his biblical perspective about the origins of life in his academic setting, he would be marked as a nonthinking person and his grades would be adversely affected.

Can you identify with the reluctance of this group? These people have no doubt that the Bible changes our personal spiritual lives, but they have not clearly understood how the Bible shapes our thinking—and can change our world.

The concerns that Matt, Michelle, Chad, and José have are real. I am not surprised when I hear that many believers don't understand a biblical worldview and that they are intimidated about being bold for Christ. We live in a time when it has become increasingly hard to sort out God's truth from Satan's deceptions. Many believers uncritically accept the views they see on television, read in books, and find on the Internet. If they are not grounded in God's Word, they can be swayed. I'm reminded of the apostle Paul's warning to "no longer be immature like children. We won't be tossed and blown about by every wind of new teaching. We will not be influenced when people try to trick us with lies so clever they sound like the truth" (Ephesians 4:14). Chaos, confusion, and compromise reign in the world today. That's why it's so essential that we study God's Word, learn what God thinks, and integrate His thoughts into every part of our lives.

Charlie, the facilitator of Matt's group, understood that truth. The night Matt posed his question to the group, Charlie said, "We need to understand that the Bible is not just about personal faith; it also speaks to how we can affect the public realm—every sphere of life—for God's glory. Scripture must touch, inform, and shape our thinking on every issue that surrounds us." He paged through his Bible for a few moments and said, "Let me read something that Jesus said about this subject." Then he read Matthew 5:13-16:

> "You are the salt of the earth. But what good is salt if it has lost its flavor? Can you make it salty again? It will be thrown out and trampled underfoot as worthless.

> "You are the light of the world—like a city on a hilltop that cannot be hidden. No one lights a lamp and then puts it under a basket. Instead, a lamp is placed on a stand, where it gives light to everyone in the house. In the same way, let your good deeds shine out for all to see, so that everyone will praise your heavenly Father."

The members of the study group were convicted by the instructions from Scripture, and they committed themselves to do two things: understand and explore the biblical worldview, and encourage each other to have an impact in their spheres of influence. For the rest of the year, they asked some hard questions: What is the biblical worldview of how we learn and what we teach? What is the biblical worldview of the sanctity of human life, especially the lives of infants who may be born prematurely and need extraordinary medical care? What is the biblical worldview of the arts and their role in reflecting God's character? What is the biblical worldview of the complexity of cellular life and the role of genetic engineering? They also prayed for and supported each other as each person tried to reflect a biblical worldview in his or her world.

The results of their Bible study, discussion, and encouragement were amazing. Not only did they find specific ways they could have an impact on significant areas, but their excitement about exploring and expressing a biblical worldview also attracted other people to join their group. Over the coming years this Bible-study group has goals of applying a biblical worldview to the areas of education, medicine, the arts, science, technology, politics, economics, law, and the environment. The Bible changes not only our personal lives but also the culture around us.

I said earlier that the Bible changes our lives in two areas: developing a biblical worldview and helping us to grow personally and spiritually. The rest of this chapter as well as the next three chapters will explore how the Bible changes our lives through our *faith* in God, through the *power* of His Spirit, through *holiness*, and through *love*.

A Warm and Vital Faith

I heard an amusing story about a group of people who met during a long drought to pray for rain. As they gathered, they discovered that only one young girl had brought an umbrella. Apparently she was the one with a vibrant faith!

The great reformer John Calvin observed, "Faith is not a distant view, but a warm embrace, of Christ, by which he dwells in us, and we are filled with the Divine Spirit."[3] I like this definition because it balances the intellectual and relational sides of faith. Faith is more than mental agreement with God; it assumes a beautiful and warm relationship with Christ. Faith must have an object—and that object is Christ. We do not merely believe in Him; we cling to Him. We began our Christian life through faith in Christ; we live our spiritual life by walking in faith.

Faith is key in our spiritual development. The Bible tells us, "So faith comes from hearing, that is, hearing the Good News about Christ" (Romans 10:17). The Bible changes our lives because it feeds and challenges our faith. And when we exercise that faith, we see the power of God.

The Old Testament is full of stories of people who responded to the words of God with faith. Remember Abraham's faith. He gave up his extended family, left his childhood home, and traveled to a place where he was a stranger, simply because he believed what God said to him. He was also willing to sacrifice his son of promise, Isaac, just because God asked him to do this. The Red Sea parted because the Israelites obeyed God's word and walked into the water, escaping certain death from Pharaoh's armies thundering behind them. The walls of Jericho collapsed because Joshua and the people responded in faith to God's word to march around the city for days and then to blow the trumpets.

What is God telling us through these stories? His message is the same as the message Jehoshaphat gave to the people before they faced a formidable enemy army: "Listen to me, all you people of Judah and Jerusalem! Believe in the LORD your God, and you will be able to stand firm. Believe in his prophets, and you will succeed" (2 Chronicles 20:20). God's message is clear: "Have faith in me, and I will show you victory."

The exercise of our faith is an eternal issue. When we build our trust in God, our belief will infuse our entire being—including the grid of our worldview—and will transform our lives. At the same time, our faith puts us in the devil's crosshairs. He realizes that if he can defeat us at the point of our faith, he will win the battle. This is devastating to our spiritual growth.

Adam and Eve found out how tragic it is not to have faith in God's word. When they first lived in the Garden of Eden, they walked and talked with God in warm fellowship. Can you imagine how wonderful that must have been? The Garden was a perfect delight; all was in harmony. They talked to God face-to-face. Who could ask for more?

But after Satan enticed Adam and Eve, they wanted more. God had planted the tree of the knowledge of good and evil at the Garden's center. God told them, "You may freely eat the fruit of every tree in the garden—except the tree of the knowledge of good and evil. If you eat its fruit, you are sure to die" (Genesis 2:16-17).

Adam and Eve were satisfied with this arrangement until Satan whispered in their ears, "You won't die...God knows that your eyes will be opened as soon as you eat it, and you will be like God, knowing both good and evil" (Genesis 3:4-5).

The temptation revolved around Adam's and Eve's faith to take God at His word. Their job was not to question God's word but to place their faith in His goodness. They needed to trust that God is all-knowing and had their best interests at heart.

But Adam and Eve doubted. They did not trust God's word. Instead, they believed the serpent's word that they would become knowledgeable, like God, if they would eat the fruit.

You know how the story ends. Adam's and Eve's lack of faith in God's provision and their disobedience brought sin into God's pristine world. They were banished from the Garden, and sin has grown and multiplied until this day.

Therefore, faith is more than the *means* by which we became children of God; it is also an *arena* where God's people, in complete dependence on Him and His Word, challenge Satan's kingdom and advance God's kingdom on earth. This is not a matter of private belief but a very public war that is waged wherever Christians exercise their faith.

We will look at six ways that the Bible changes our lives by challenging us to exercise our faith.

Walk with God by Faith

The issue of faith for Charissa was the loss of income. She and her husband, Luke, had discussed their options many times. They had two toddlers, Hunter and Heather, and Hunter just wasn't thriving in the day-care facility. In fact, he was developing an aggressive streak that worried his parents. Charissa and Luke discussed the problem and prayed about it, but they also studied the Bible together to try to discern God's will for their family. They read passages about teaching, disciplining, and nurturing their children. The couple finally came to the conclusion that the Lord was leading them to intervene in their son's life by having Charissa quit her job as a lawyer and become a stay-at-home mom. But Charissa made a sizable income, and the couple had never had to live on one salary. They'd have to completely revise their lifestyle.

Just the thought of restricting themselves to a much lower income gave Charissa the shakes. She loved her morning cappuccinos at Starbucks, her power lunches at least once a week, and shopping for her business wardrobe. Her parents had provided her with everything she needed before she married, and she and Luke had done well too. It would be a big step of faith for her to live on a limited budget.

But faith requires more than one step; it is a lifestyle. What Charissa didn't realize at the time is that God wants to walk us through every situation step by step. Have you ever taken a stroll with a dear friend along the beach or on a mountain trail? It isn't the first step or the last that makes the trip memorable, but the fellowship along the way. That's how God wants us to approach our walk of faith.

For Charissa, the first step—quitting her job—was indeed a big one. But she also faced other steps every day—saying no to that cappuccino, praying over the bills as they came in, asking God to lead her and Luke to develop a reasonable budget, searching the Bible for guidelines for new personal priorities. What she found was that the Scriptures shaped her faith and her faith walk was a truly rich experience.

Produce Fruit by Faith

I have often been asked, "What was your greatest act of faith?" According to the apostle Paul, faith is a gift from God (Ephesians 2:8-10), so I cannot take credit for even the smallest act of faith on my part. It all goes to God's glory. But I will say that the purchase of the Arrowhead Springs Conference Center in California in 1961 required great faith. We knew the property would be perfect for our ministry, but the price was a whopping two million dollars. The ministry, which was quite small in those days, had almost no money. How would we do it? The other ministry leaders and I studied the Bible and prayed until we were certain that we were going in the direction God wanted for the ministry.

Because we were sure that God had called us to buy the property, I had God's peace that He would provide the funds needed to make the payments. From a human point of view, I could see no way that this could be possible. But the other leaders and I had complete confidence that God would show us a miracle. And He did. We were able to borrow fifteen thousand dollars for a down payment, and we closed the deal.

We found out that faith always produces peace. When you know that what you are doing is what God asks, no matter how impossible it seems, the peace of God always accompanies the decision. None of us could naturally turn our concerns over to God and have peace. That was a fruit produced by the Holy Spirit within us.

In addition to having peace, our acts of faith will be contagious. Over the years, many people have said things such as, "Because you did what you did in purchasing Arrowhead Springs, we had the faith to believe God for something big for ourselves."

Surrender Your Will by Faith

As a young believer, I was influenced by a verse from the Sermon on the Mount: "Blessed are those who hunger and thirst for righteousness, for they will be filled" (Matthew 5:6 NIV). I hungered and thirsted after righteousness with all my heart. I spent long days of fasting and prayer, crying out to God for His power to be released in and through my life. Then God graciously answered me by helping me to understand that the emotional experience I was seeking was not His priority for me. Through my study of the Bible, I realized He was calling me to live a life of faith as an act of my will in obedience to His commands.

This is a hard concept to grasp in our culture. We have been taught that experience is the priority in life. We search for a career that makes us happy. We marry because we feel romantic love. We develop relationships with people who make us feel good.

God does not devalue emotions. Sometimes feelings are the way that God gets our attention, moves us, and makes us aware of His presence. But experiences and emotions are unreliable. They change and cannot be sustained. They also can lead us in the wrong direction. God wants us to enjoy our emotions, but He expects us to build our faith on our will.

God's Word changed me and helped me to see that He wanted me to surrender my will to Him. When I did that, I drew on the supernatural resources that are available to me through Christ. My hunger and thirst were fulfilled, and I have enjoyed many wonderful years of adventurous walking with Christ.

Unlock the Supernatural Through Faith

God is in the business of providing miracles as a result of our faith. Our new birth is a miracle. Our growth in Christ is supernatural. In addition, many amazing events will happen to us when we place our faith in Christ.

In the New Testament, Jesus says to His disciples: "I tell you the truth, if you have faith and don't doubt, you can do things like this and much more. You can even say to this mountain, 'May you be lifted up and thrown into the sea,' and it will happen. You can pray for anything, and if you have faith, you will receive it" (Matthew 21:21-22). Many times in the history of Campus Crusade for Christ I have seen God use passages like this one to challenge our staff to exercise our faith and watch Him work. When the Iron Curtain fell more than a decade ago, the Lord opened up a new field of ministry for us. From the early days of our work, Vonette and I have had a special prayer burden for the Russian people, so when staff members were able to bring God's Word into that former atheistic country, my heart was overflowing with joy. God expanded our ministry all across Russia, and we saw miracles happen everywhere.

One story of how the Bible changes lives especially touches my heart. As opportunities to bring the gospel to people all over Russia began multiplying, teams of staff members armed with the *JESUS* film (the story of Jesus taken from the book of Luke), Bibles, and other literature spread all through that marvelous country. Eventually, a team reached Stravopol. But when they arrived to hold conferences, they discovered that they couldn't get a shipload of Bibles delivered from Moscow in time for the meeting. This would seriously hamper the team's mission to give Bibles to the spiritually hungry people of the city.

The team members exercised their faith. They prayed, asking God to use supernatural means to help them get the Bibles in time. A local resident mentioned that at one time the government had a warehouse full of Bibles right outside the city. In the 1930s Stalin had ordered a purge of all Bibles and believers in the area. In Stravopol, this edict was carried out with a vengeance. Thousands of Bibles were confiscated, and many believers were sent to Russian prison camps. The Bibles had been ordered to be destroyed, but instead they were stashed in a warehouse—and forgotten until the man heard of the team's need. Were the Bibles still there after several decades? Were they waiting for just the moment when the people of Stravopol could once again treasure God's Word in the open?

After much prayer, one team member went to the government officials and asked about the Bibles. Not only were the Bibles still in the warehouse, but the team was also given permission to take them and use them for the conference.

The team members were thrilled. They hired a few Russian workers and rented a truck to load up the Bibles and take them to the convention center. One of the workers was a hostile young man, an agnostic college student who had just come for the day's wages. He had no time for God.

As the Bibles were being loaded, this young man disappeared. The team members were puzzled. But eventually they found him crying in a corner of the warehouse. When they asked him what was wrong, he told an amazing story. He had slipped away from the group to steal a Bible for himself. What he found shook him to his knees. Out of the thousands of Bibles in the warehouse, the one he picked up had a handwritten signature inside the cover. That Bible had belonged to his grandmother—a woman who had been persecuted for her faith all her life. No doubt she had prayed for her family and their spiritual welfare many times. The young man's discovery of his grandmother's Bible made God real to him. He took the Bible home with him, began reading it, and it transformed his life.[4]

Miracles are one of the most powerful tools God uses to smash Satan's strongholds and give unquestioned and credible testimony to the fact that He alone is God. Look at Hebrews 11, where you will find many examples of people who were "heroes of the faith." These stories are presented in chronological order, beginning with Abel, the son of Adam and Eve. Forty verses later, the reader has been soaked in miracle after miracle performed by God in response to absolute trust in His inerrant, infallible, and authoritative Word. And God's miraculous power is no less powerful today than it was then.

Achieve Victory by Faith

Most of us seek mountaintop spiritual experiences. Recently I was reading the autobiography of a friend who talked about how as a Christian leader he had lived on the mountain peaks all his life. He rejoiced in those experiences until he went through an unbelievably difficult period that lasted for years.

He was devastated. His friends deserted him. His life was destroyed. His ministry was in chaos. Although his initial response to the trials was to sink into depression, God helped him, and soon he experienced a supernatural peace.

In the apostle Peter's letters to new believers in Asia, he challenged them:

> There is wonderful joy ahead, even though you must endure many trials for a little while. These trials will show that your faith is genuine. It is being tested as fire tests and purifies gold—though your faith is far more precious than mere gold. So when your faith remains strong through many trials, it will bring you much praise and glory and honor on the day when Jesus Christ is revealed to the whole world (1 Peter 1:6-7).

Did you catch the relationship of trials and faith? Trials test our faith, and our faith is inestimably valuable to God.

My friend clung to passages like this one as he persevered through his trials. He began to know the joy of the Lord and the fulfillment of His promises in a new dimension. Now my friend looks back over those devastating years of heartache, sorrow, and humiliation and remembers that it is in the valleys where one finds the sweet fruit trees and flowers of life.

Most people seek mountaintop experiences with God. But we often forget that real mountaintops are usually barren because plant life does not grow freely at elevated heights. Likewise, spiritual mountaintops, though pleasurable for a time, are not places where believers grow. We must therefore recognize the fallacy of seeking emotional experiences and spiritual highs, and instead rejoice in what God is doing in our lives through trials, knowing that trials are His way of refining us.

Our faith in the midst of trials can produce amazing results. When the Thessalonian believers were enduring persecution, the apostle Paul wrote to encourage them, "We proudly tell God's other churches about your endurance and faithfulness in all the persecutions and hardships you are suffering" (2 Thessalonians 1:4). Our overcoming faith will make a public declaration of God's faithfulness and glory.

As I mentioned before, when I was a new believer, I faced a temptation that could have destroyed my faith. The Bible changed my life as it grounded me in the truth of what was happening: "The temptations in your life are no different from what others experience. And God is faithful. He will not allow the temptation to be more than you can stand. When you are tempted, he will show you a way out so that you can endure" (1 Corinthians 10:13). I memorized that verse and clung to it as I claimed its promise. God dramatically kept His Word at that time in my life as He has on similar occasions through the years.

I have learned that when a temptation comes, I say to the Lord Jesus, "I can't handle this temptation. I surrender to You." Then by faith I claim the promise from His Word. No matter what the nature of the temptation, God deals with it. I thank Him for taking care of it—for carrying the load for me. God's Word strengthens my faith and changes my life.

Thank God in Faith

Some years ago, my personal world seemed to be crumbling around me. All that I had worked and planned for in the ministry of Campus Crusade for Christ was hanging by a slender thread as we faced a financial crisis that could bankrupt the movement. The crisis we faced could result in the loss of our beautiful facilities at Arrowhead Springs, where we were already training thousands of disciples. I thought, *God, were we wrong to buy Arrowhead Springs in faith?*

Once again God's Word gave me direction. "Don't worry about anything; instead, pray about everything. Tell God what you need, and thank Him for all He has done. Then you will experience God's peace, which exceeds anything we can understand. His peace will guard your hearts and minds as you live in Christ Jesus" (Philippians 4:6-7). That passage grounded me, giving me directions for how I must approach the crisis. So when the word came to me that everything was virtually lost, I fell to my knees and began to praise the Lord.

As I thanked God in the midst of this crisis, His supernatural peace flooded my heart, just as the Bible promised. I felt assured that He would provide the miracle we needed. In a matter of a few days, totally apart from any of my own abilities to solve the problem, God brought the right people into the right circumstances with the funds to save Arrowhead Springs for the ministry. Only God could have worked this miracle. He was simply keeping His promise and honoring the faith of His children.

When you face crises in your lives, choose to thank God rather than be afraid. You will discover that when you express faith through thanksgiving, obedience, and gratitude to God, He will release His great power on your behalf and He will enable you to be more fruitful for Him. Memorize Scripture verses that will strengthen your faith. When God's Word saturates your mind, your faith is strengthened.

Offering thanks to God in the midst of crises requires a sacrifice of the will. Friend, do not wait until you feel like thanking God. Thank Him as an act of your will. When you acknowledge your faith in Him through your attitude of thanksgiving, even though circumstances suggest there is no hope, God will release miraculous power on your behalf. He turns tragedy into triumph, discord to harmony, and defeat to victory.

Faith opens the door to one of God's attributes—His power. Just what can we do when we are filled with God's Spirit through faith? In the next chapter, we will discover how unlimited our horizons are when we see the world as God sees it and act in faith.

DISCOVER THE TREASURE

The Bible studies in part 4 will introduce a new map—the 4Ts—as well as the third kind of Bible study, the biographical or character study. Let me explain the new map. The 4Ts are Then, Timeless, Today, To me.

Then:

Perspective: What is the historical and/or cultural setting and background of the passage? (Discover this first from the passage itself, but you may also want to check a Bible dictionary, study notes in a study Bible, or other resources to understand historical details about the setting and background.)

People: Who are the principal characters? Observe their ages, roles, positions, status in society—anything that will help you understand who the people are. What role does faith play in their story? What are their strengths and weaknesses? What growth in maturity did you observe? Who influences these characters, and whom do they influence? What problems did the characters encounter? (Again, discover what you can from the passage itself. *After* you are finished with your personal study, you may want to consult a Bible dictionary or study notes, but don't let those do your thinking for you.)

Timeless:

Preview: What is the main focus of each chapter?

Principles: What are the most important lessons to be learned? What do they teach about the Father, Son, and Holy Spirit?

Today:

Purpose for today: How do the timeless truths apply to today's society?

Pattern: How are the people and situations the same today as they were in Bible times?

To me:

Promises: What possible promises can I claim from this passage?

Practical application: What example do the characters set for me? Does the passage convict me of a sin I need to confess?

Prayer: Is there a prayer for me to echo?

Let's practice this map by doing a biographical study of the Old Testament prophet Daniel, who exercised his faith when he faced some pressured decisions and consequences. We'll limit our study to the exciting drama recounted in the first six chapters of the book of Daniel. In your Bible-study notebook, write out your responses to each question below. Then record your prayer points.

Read Daniel 1:1–6:28.

Then:

Perspective: What is the historical and cultural setting and background of the passage? What has just happened in Jerusalem? In what location does most of the action in the passage take place? How do the Babylonians and God's people differ in their customs and religious practices? What role do those cultural differences play in the drama that unfolds in these chapters? (Discover this first from the passage itself, but you may also want to check a Bible dictionary, study notes in a study Bible, or other resources to understand historical details about the setting and background.)

People: Who are the principal characters? What are their ages, roles, positions, and status? What role does faith play in Daniel's story? What are his strengths and weaknesses? What growth in maturity did you observe? What problems did he encounter, and how did he handle the problem? Who influenced Daniel, and whom did he influence? (Again, discover what you can from the passage itself. *After* you are finished with your personal study, you may want to consult a Bible dictionary or study notes, but don't let those do your thinking for you.)

Timeless:

Preview: What is the main focus of each chapter?

Principles: What are the most important lessons to be learned? What do they teach about the Father, Son, and Holy Spirit?

Today:

Purpose for today: How do the timeless truths apply to today's society?

Pattern: How are the people and situations the same today as they were in Bible times?

To me:

Promises: What possible promises can I claim from this passage?

Practical application: What example do the characters set for me? Does the passage convict me of a sin I need to confess?

Prayer: Is there a prayer for me to echo?

Prayer Points:

14

How Does the Bible Connect Me to God's Power?

Sometimes Laura had a hard time getting up in the morning and preparing to go to work. A supervisor at a county agency, she was responsible for thirty employees. Every week it seemed as if personnel problems snarled at her: workers had disputes with each other; people tried to bend the office rules to gain personal advantage; others failed to live up to their responsibilities. Laura felt as if she was inadequate to play the mediator in these situations. And even more difficult, many times workers came to her with personal crises and asked her for advice.

Laura felt her main goal in her job was to represent her Savior and Lord. Although she was prohibited from aggressively sharing her faith during work hours, she looked for opportunities to point people to God. But she hadn't made much progress in introducing others to Christ. Most people were satisfied with their spiritual lives and were tolerant but not open to her views. Sometimes Laura wondered why God had put her in her job. She didn't know of even one other believer in her building.

Then the county announced that the budget was in serious trouble, so cuts would be made across the board. Immediately, the tension in the office heightened to monumental proportions. Single mothers worried about losing their only source of income. Workers with high levels of personal debt fretted over the threat of being demoted or even laid off. Tension and disagreements between coworkers increased.

One of the ways Laura prepared to handle the day's stress was to lean on the promises of Scripture. Each morning before work, she took ten minutes to read a verse of Scripture and pray about it. She then placed her concerns in God's hands and asked Him to give her grace and patience. That was the only way she could survive the tumult she encountered during the workday. God honored her request and gave her an unusual calm when others were distraught.

The crisis went on for weeks. Rumors flew around the office about who was likely to be laid off or whose jobs might be terminated. The traffic in and out of Laura's office increased. Amazingly, she discovered that employees who once had no time to talk to her now seemed attracted to her faith. In one week she had more people ask about faith issues than she had had in the previous year.

Finally the pink slips appeared in employees' mailboxes. A few received nothing; others found themselves without a job. Demotions and transfers were numerous. Several people cried openly in the office. The atmosphere was thick with despair.

Laura received her own pink slip. She not only had been assigned to another office twenty miles away, but she also had been demoted to a nonsupervisory position. The news hit her like glass on cement. But she knew that this was her opportunity to live in God's power. The first thing she did was to take out her Bible and read two passages from Philippians:

> For God is working in you, giving you the desire and the power to do what pleases him. Do everything without complaining and arguing, so that no one can criticize you. Live clean, innocent lives as children of God, shining like bright lights in a world full of crooked and perverse people (Philippians 2:13-15).

> Don't worry about anything; instead, pray about everything. Tell God what you need, and thank him for all he has done. Then you will experience God's peace, which exceeds anything we can understand. His peace will guard your hearts and minds as you live in Christ Jesus (Philippians 4:6-7).

She clung to two promises: that God was working in her, giving her the power to do what pleases Him; and that if she surrendered her cares to God, she would experience His peace. As she continued on through her day, she found herself praying and remembering those verses often, sometimes even second by second.

Over the next three weeks, she was able to influence the morale of the people in the office. Her coworkers stopped by, one by one, to talk. Invariably, they all asked in one way or another, "How can you be so cool when the situation is so bad?"

That was just the opening she needed to share her faith in Christ. Many of the workers seemed quite interested in what she had to say. One woman admitted that she was not seeking God with her whole heart. She thanked Laura for showing her the importance of her faith in God. Laura led another woman to faith in Christ, a single mom who wanted to bring her children to Laura's church.

When the time arrived for Laura to leave her office for her new position, she was sad, but she had hope in the midst of her adjustments. She had experienced God's power and His peace, and she knew that God would bless her in the same way in her new job.

One of the secrets to the power and peace Laura experienced was that she read the Word and allowed Scripture to change the way she thought and responded. Romans 12:2 says, "Don't copy the behavior and customs of this world, but let God transform you into a new person by changing the way you think." Through her study of the Bible, Laura discovered not only the character of God but also the power to reflect God's character in the way she lived. When the crisis hit, people saw the peace with which she handled the situation, and they were attracted by it. When we have a biblical worldview—seeing the world through God's eyes—we become more like Christ.

Like Laura, you and I may feel very ordinary at times, but Christ's power in us makes all the difference. The Bible promises,

> But those who trust in the LORD will find new strength.
> They will soar high on wings like eagles.

They will run and not grow weary.
They will walk and not faint.
(Isaiah 40:31)

Our amazing God masterfully weaves His power around our fumbling efforts. Often we feel powerless, but we must always remember that the source of all power is the Master of the universe. His power is available to all who seek Him.

Our Resources for Spiritual Power

Think about what happens when we board a jet. We say, "I'm flying to my destination." But we are not doing the flying, the plane is. We are able to fly only because we are on the plane. If we stepped outside the door, we would plummet to the ground.

In a similar way, we have no power in and of ourselves to live the Christian life. It requires supernatural power—Christ's power. We can have that power only when Christ lives in and through us. If we try to "step out of the plane" and live the Christian life in our own strength, we will fail. But the Bible assures us, "By his divine power, God has given us everything we need for living a godly life. We have received all of this by coming to know him, the one who called us to himself by means of his marvelous glory and excellence" (2 Peter 1:3).

All believers have three sources of spiritual power: the Holy Spirit, the Bible, and prayer. These three elements combine in an awesome way to give us power. They all work together. We are empowered by the Holy Spirit who lives in us. He is the source of all spiritual power. He gives us the power to live a supernatural life and be fruitful for God. "But you will receive power when the Holy Spirit comes upon you. And you will be my witnesses, telling people about me everywhere— in Jerusalem, throughout Judea, in Samaria, and to the ends of the earth" (Acts 1:8).

We are also empowered by God's Word. "For the word of God is alive and powerful" (Hebrews 4:12). The Holy Spirit transforms our lives as we study and read God's Word. We cannot separate the Spirit's power from the Bible's influence in our lives. They go hand in hand.

The Bible teaches us God's truth, and the Spirit helps us interpret and apply the Word to our lives.

Prayer is our response to God as we are led by the Spirit and are taught by the Word. In fact, the combination of the Spirit's work in us and the Bible's truth leads inevitably to a life of prayer. Prayer releases God's power in our lives. Colossians 4:2 commands, "Devote yourselves to prayer with an alert mind and a thankful heart." God wants us to use His power for His purposes today.

Power for Victory

If someone asked you what the natural vehicles of power are in the world today, what would you answer? You might suggest wealth, authority, popularity, might, and influence. If people have one of these qualities, they will attract more of the others.

But God's power is not limited by our abilities, resources, or intelligence. God's power is supernatural. Time and physical barriers do not bind Him. His power can be awesome (as displayed in the parting of the Red Sea) or serene (as demonstrated by Jesus's healing hand on the eyes of the blind man).

The greatest proof of God's power was shown in the death and resurrection of Jesus Christ. What kind of strength was involved in the Easter story? There is the power of love that sent Jesus to die for unworthy sinners. There is the power of justice that was exacted in Christ's suffering rather than ours. There is the power of Christ, who laid down His life and took it up again of His own accord. The sacrificial act of Christ on the cross defeated death and Satan, making it possible for us to have eternal fellowship with our all-powerful God.

The Bible tells us that the same power that raised Christ from the dead now lives in us, His people (Ephesians 1:19-20). What an amazing reality. Because of God's power in us, we are not limited by our natural resources. Because of God's power in us, we have power beyond our own intelligence or wealth. If we understand who we are in Christ, we can access His power to reach our spiritual potential. Through Him, we can reach heights we could never attain on our own.

Power for Proclaiming the Gospel

For eight years Jonelle had been trying to share her faith with her neighbor, a Japanese widow. Tokiko was satisfied with her Buddhist religion, and each time Jonelle raised the subject of faith in Jesus Christ, Tokiko said, "You're a Christian, and I'm a Buddhist. I don't want to talk about it."

Jonelle kept witnessing to Tokiko through her way of life—the ways she helped her neighbor and treated her like a friend—but nothing seemed to change. After years of rejection, Jonelle was discouraged and had a hard time bringing up the subject again.

One day when she was studying her Bible, she came across a verse with a promise that she needed: "The Lord isn't really being slow about his promise, as some people think. No, he is being patient for your sake. He does not want anyone to be destroyed, but wants everyone to repent" (2 Peter 3:9). Jonelle was comforted by the verse and claimed the promise that God loved Tokiko and was giving her time to come to Him.

At two o'clock one morning Jonelle was awakened by a phone call. It was Tokiko calling to say she was having a heart attack. Jonelle got dressed and ran over to her neighbor's house. The ambulance came and rushed Tokiko to the local hospital.

Jonelle visited Tokiko every day during her hospitalization. During one evening's visit, Jonelle felt prompted to speak to Tokiko about her eternal destiny, especially since Tokiko's health was precarious. But Jonelle was afraid of being rejected once again.

As she pulled up a chair closer to Tokiko's bed, Jonelle began praying silently, *Lord, in my Bible reading this morning Your Word said that Your Holy Spirit would help me be Your witness. Give me the boldness to talk with her.*

But no opportunity came. As the two women visited, the second hand on the clock over the bed ticked loudly. Visiting hours would soon be over and Jonelle would have to leave. She prayed silently again, *Lord, I know You don't want Tokiko to perish without knowing You. I'm claiming that promise for Tokiko.*

Just as she finished praying, Tokiko said, "I had a dream last night. I dreamt that God was talking to me, but I couldn't hear what He was saying."

Jonelle broke out in a big smile. With boldness and confidence she explained the plan of salvation to her neighbor, and before visiting hours were over, Tokiko had prayed, asking Christ to be her Savior. The two women hugged and cried for joy.

Jonelle experienced the truth of Christ's promise to His followers: "When the Holy Spirit has come upon you, you will receive power and will tell people about Me everywhere" (Acts 1:8). God has empowered us to be His witnesses, even in the most difficult circumstances. Words apart from the power of God are simply words. But as we draw on His power, the gospel will penetrate the minds and hearts of those around us.

Power to Overcome Evil Forces

One of the dreams of my life's ministry was to help produce a film about the life of Christ, a film that could win millions to Christ. Through a series of miraculous events and God's perfect timing, Campus Crusade produced the *JESUS* film, which has been used throughout the world to reach people for Christ. The film is based on the story of Jesus, and the dialogue and text are very close to the text of the book of Luke.

Daniel Atayaye was part of a *JESUS* film team in Nigeria and showed the film to radical Muslims in the northern part of the country. Many of these Muslims had never read the Bible or heard the message of the gospel.

One day as the team was traveling to a village to show the film, it encountered hostile opposition. Young Muslim men threw a huge rock at the car, shattering the windshield. Glass flew everywhere, and the car ran off the road. A big shard sliced open the driver's arm, and several bits of glass flew into Daniel's eyes.

The local police arrived and took the team members to the police station for medical aid. They told the team that they had caught the young men who had thrown the rock. The police wanted Daniel and his team to stay and press charges. But doing this meant that the team would miss the opportunity to show the film that night. In addition, the doctor wanted to remove the glass splinters from Daniel's eyes right away. If not taken care of, the damage could cause blindness.

But emboldened by his commitment to the Bible's instructions to "go into all the world and preach the Good News to everyone" (Mark 16:15), Daniel decided to press on. "We have been praying to go to this village, and many things have tried to stop us. We must go now; we won't wait. I will just pray that God will protect me so we can go and show the film."

The team left and reached the village in time for the gathering. Several hundred people received Christ that night.

Later, Daniel was able to sleep soundly in spite of the glass in his eyes. He describes what happened the next morning when he woke up. "I blinked my eyes and looked in the mirror. I saw two little pieces of glass in the corner of my eyes. I brushed them out with my little finger, and my eyes were just fine. God took care of me."[5]

The team saw God's power not only as the Word of God touched the hearts of the people through the film but also as they experienced the reality of the promise found in 1 John 5:4: "For every child of God defeats this evil world, and we achieve this victory through our faith." Neither the hostile young men nor the physical problems could keep the team from what God led them to do. God's power working in and through us surpasses all worldly and evil forces. This is what gave Daniel's team the power to keep going—and what can give us the same power.

Power to Withstand Adversity and Temptation

People traveling through the Midwest in the spring and summer often see the abundant pink wild roses lining the roadsides. These are some of the hardiest plants on the prairie. Even though their petals look fragile, the plant survives tremendous natural adversity. In the winter the plant endures temperatures up to thirty degrees below zero in the northern parts of the Midwest, yet the wild rose happily blooms in the spring. Years of drought don't kill it. Neither do the many days of searing hot sun. As long as the wild rose has its roots planted in the prairie soil, it spreads and grows abundantly.

But you can't pick prairie roses, put them in a vase, and decorate your table. The flowers immediately wilt and turn brown. And the plant doesn't grow well in the pampered soil of a garden.

This is a picture of our life in Christ. As long as we are rooted in God's Word, we have the power to endure all kinds of adversity and temptation. But if we are removed from our source of truth, our moral stance wilts.

When facing temptation and trials, remember the many promises of Scripture and rely on the Holy Spirit to empower you. The apostle James encourages us: "Dear brothers and sisters, when troubles of any kind come your way, consider it an opportunity for great joy. For you know that when your faith is tested, your endurance has a chance to grow. So let it grow, for when your endurance is fully developed, you will be perfect and complete, needing nothing" (James 1:2-4). Then stand firm.

I encourage you to use your Bible as your source of power. It's the *only* way to live. This power will enable us to recognize what is right and to live a holy life, which is the subject of our next chapter.

DISCOVER THE TREASURE

For this study, you will study an entire book of the Bible, a relatively short one: the book of Esther. The story of Esther is the story of spiritual power that overcame the forces of evil. Since the book of Esther has ten short chapters, you may want to do this study over a few days' time. Divide up the book in a way that makes sense to you, but be sure to coordinate all the ideas as you work along and to review all the chapters at the end to find the main truths in the book. As you study the character of Esther, you will learn more about God's power available to you.

For this biographical study of a book of the Bible, you will again use the 4Ts map: **Then, Timeless, Today, To me.**

Then:

Perspective: What is the historical and cultural setting and background of the passage? Where and when does the story take place? How does the culture of this place differ from the Jewish culture? How is that significant in the story? What are the contemporary names for the cities and areas mentioned in this book? What is the spiritual/emotional setting of the book? (Discover this first from the passage itself, but you may also want to check a Bible dictionary, study notes in a study Bible, or other resources to understand historical details about the setting and background.)

People: Who are the principal characters? Observe their ages, roles, positions, status in society—anything that will help you understand who the people are. How strong is their faith? How significant is it that one of the main characters is a woman who needs to stand up to men? What problems did the characters encounter? (Again, discover what you can from the passage itself. *After* you are finished with your personal study, you may want to consult a Bible dictionary or study notes, but don't let those do your thinking for you.)

Timeless:

Preview: What is the main focus of each chapter?

Principles: What are the most important lessons to be learned? What do they teach about the Father, Son, and Holy Spirit?

Today:

Purpose for today: How do the timeless truths apply to today's society?

Pattern: How are the people and situations the same today as they were in Bible times?

To me:

Promises: What possible promises can I claim from this passage?

Practical application: What example do the characters set for me? Does the passage convict me of a sin I need to confess?

Prayer: Is there a prayer for me to echo?

Prayer Points:

15

How Does the Bible Help Me Live a Holy Life?

God wants us to live holy lives. We have no doubts about that. But just what does that mean? How can we understand what a holy life looks like?

The Bible gives us a detailed picture of holiness. Before Christ was born, people needed a way to understand who God is and what He expected of them. So God instituted a form of worship that pictured God's plans for history and His requirements for holy living. We read that picture in the Old Testament.

Here's how it all began. After the Israelites' exodus from the oppression under Egyptian rulers, they wandered in the wilderness on their way to the new land God promised to give them. The Israelites had never lived on their own before, so God began showing them how to live as a nation. At the center of their national life was worship of God.

God instructed the people to build a worship center, a Tabernacle. It was a house of worship made like a large tent so that it could be moved right along with the people. The structure and furnishings of the Tabernacle were a visual way of teaching the people about their relationship to God and the future Messiah, Jesus Christ.

God's Picture of Holiness

Travel with me back to the sandy trail through the wilderness and examine the Tabernacle and its form of worship. First, you will see that all around the Tabernacle was a curtained fence that kept the people out (Exodus 27:9-18). This curtain was made of fine linen, and it reminded the people of God's holiness and righteousness. The curtain separated the people from the place where God dwelled, just as sin separates us from a holy God.

Looking over the curtain, we can see a taller structure that looks like a tent. Amazingly, the tent walls were made of plain brown goatskin (Exodus 26:14). That's probably not what you expect of a house of worship. Most churches and synagogues are gorgeous or ostentatious. But the plain brown skins picture Jesus Christ. He came as a little baby, not as a king or grand philosopher. Isaiah 53:2 says of the Messiah, "There was nothing beautiful or majestic about his appearance, nothing to attract us to him." Jesus looked so ordinary that people of His day did not recognize Him as the Son of God.

But underneath the goatskin was a covering of ram skins, dyed red (Exodus 26:14 NIV). Of course, that symbolized Christ's blood, the only remedy for our sin. Under the red layer was a covering of sheets made from goat hair (Exodus 26:7-13). If you were an Israelite, you would remember that once a year a goat, a scapegoat, was sacrificed for the sins of the people (Leviticus 16:6-10). Once again, we see a picture of Jesus Christ. Then the last layer on the underside was a linen cloth, decorated with cherubim embroidered with yarn dyed red, blue, and purple (Exodus 26:1-6). The priests who came inside the Tabernacle would look up and see the angels, another reminder of God's holiness. The colors also pointed to Jesus: red was the color of the blood of the sacrifice; purple was the color of royalty; and blue signified heaven.

Are you amazed at how precisely God pictured His holiness? But the furniture and the worship activities held inside the curtains also speak of God's holiness.

First, we go through the only door in the curtained fence, symbolizing that Jesus is the door, the only way to God. Only the priests were allowed to go in, so we'll have to put ourselves in the shoes of a holy man of Israel. Right inside the door we come to a bronze altar. To proceed farther into the worship area, we have to sacrifice a lamb for our own sins. The animal was a symbol of how Christ died in our place for our sin and how we must be born again to approach God.

Next we find a bronze laver (like a large bowl), and it is so shiny that it acts like a mirror. It is filled with water. We must wash our hands and feet in the laver (Exodus 30:17-21). This represents the cleansing that Christians do when they recognize their sins and confess them daily to God.

Now we are ready to go inside the Tabernacle walls. As we enter, we find two compartments: the Holy Place and the Most Holy Place. Glancing around the Holy Place, we see a lampstand, or candlestick, on the left. It has three branches on each side and one in the middle (Exodus 25:31-40). Its cups are filled with oil and are continuously burning. The lampstand reminds us that Jesus is the light of the world. On the right is a table with twelve loaves of bread, called the Bread of the Presence, one loaf for each of the tribes of Israel (Exodus 25:23-30; Leviticus 24:5-6). This reminds us that Jesus is the Bread of Life. Behind these two pieces is the incense altar (Exodus 30:1-9). On it burns sweet incense, a reminder of our prayers going up to God.

The final place is the Most Holy Place, or Holy of Holies, which is hidden from view by a huge floor-to-ceiling veil or curtain (Exodus 26:31-33). The curtain separates us from the holiest place on earth, which is where God dwells. Only the high priest could enter the Most Holy Place, and he could enter it only once a year. He had to bring a blood sacrifice with him as a payment for his sins. That's how serious God is about keeping His presence pure and holy. While this place was off-limits to all the people of Israel except the high priest, Christians now have access to God's holy presence. When Christ was crucified, the veil of the Temple was split in two from top to bottom (Mark 15:38; Luke 23:45). Today we have access to God's holy presence because of Christ's sacrifice (Hebrews 6:19-20).

The high priest entered through the veil. Inside the Most Holy Place was only one piece of furniture: the Ark of the Covenant (Exodus 25:10-16). It was a golden box that contained Aaron's staff, a piece of manna, and the tablets with the Ten Commandments written on them (Hebrews 9:4). On top of the Ark was a slab of gold with two cherubim on each side looking down at it. It was called the atonement cover (Exodus 25:17-22). This is where God resided, on the atonement cover or the mercy seat, as some translations call it. The high priest put the blood of the sacrifice on the atonement cover. Once again, we see the picture of God's greatest sacrifice.

Do you see how carefully God has pictured His holiness? The Old Testament Tabernacle and mode of worship foreshadows the relationship we have with God now because of our holy High Priest, Jesus Christ. To read a beautiful summary of this relationship, read Hebrews 8 through 10.

God's Holiness in Us

If holiness is that important to God, you can see why He wants us to live holy lives. We must not underestimate the urgency of holiness. Quoting the Old Testament, the apostle Peter writes, "For the Scriptures say, 'You must be holy because I am holy'" (1 Peter 1:16). This is not a suggestion; it is a command. We are called to holy living because God is holy; indeed, His very name is holy. As Mary, the mother of Jesus, said, "for the Mighty One has done great things for me—holy is his name" (Luke 1:49 NIV).

By God's grace, I have longed to be a holy man ever since I met Him in 1945. Through the reading of God's Word, prayer, and seeking to obey Him, the pursuit of holiness continues to be one of the most important goals of my life. The Bible calls this process *sanctification.*

If we are to live holy lives, we must consider our bodies to be the temple of God. The apostle Paul writes, "Don't you realize that all of you together are the temple of God and that the Spirit of God lives in you? God will destroy anyone who destroys this temple. For God's temple is holy, and you are that temple" (1 Corinthians 3:16-17). The body of Christ has replaced the Most Holy Place because God the Holy Spirit dwells in us as believers. As a result, we are to offer our bodies before God in holiness. Paul says elsewhere, "And so, dear brothers and sisters, I plead with you to give your bodies to God because of all he has done for you. Let them be a living and holy sacrifice—the kind he will find acceptable. This is truly the way to worship him" (Romans 12:1). It is our obedience to God's command to be holy that makes us "living stones that God is building into his spiritual temple. What's more, you are his holy priests. Through the mediation of Jesus Christ, you offer spiritual sacrifices that please God" (1 Peter 2:5).

Experiencing a Life of Holiness

Clearly, God considers living a life of holiness to be extremely important. M.R. DeHaan, a famous radio Bible teacher, used a helpful illustration to communicate the value of holiness. A bar of steel worth $5 can yield any of the following: If it is made into horseshoes, it will be worth $10. If it is made into needles, the value becomes $350. If it is made into delicate springs for expensive watches, it will yield $250,000. We are like the $5 bar of steel. Our commitment to holiness will determine whether we become Christians of minimal, moderate, or significant spiritual influence.[6]

We cannot become holy through self-effort but only through the power of the Holy Spirit. From the very beginning of my new life as a believer, I really worked at being a Christian. I attended church several times each week, and I was even elected the president of a young-adult group of almost one thousand college and postcollege people. I studied and memorized Scripture, lived a disciplined life of prayer, and witnessed for Christ regularly. Yet, the harder I tried to live the Christian life, the more frustrated I became.

No one can become holy by trying. Only as we depend on Jesus Christ as the source of our holiness and know we are complete in Him can we begin to experience this life of holiness. We can look back at the worship pattern in the Tabernacle to see how we are to offer our spiritual sacrifices.

1. We must keep ourselves separate from sin. No sin was allowed to mar the Most Holy Place. In the same way, we are to avoid all sin and even the appearance of evil. God instructs believers to *live* in holiness before God. This truth is rooted in the Old Testament, where God calls people to separate themselves for service: "In this way, you will set the Levites apart from the rest of the people of Israel, and the Levites will belong to me" (Numbers 8:14). Priests were to consecrate themselves and keep themselves free from sin. Today, a spiritual separation applies to *all* believers, which the New Testament calls the "priesthood of the believer." John writes, "He has made us a Kingdom of priests for God his Father" (Revelation 1:6).

2. *We must confess our sins immediately.* The reason the laver was polished so finely was to reflect the image of the person standing in front of it, the person who came to wash his hands and feet. This is a picture of examining ourselves with the help of the Holy Spirit and confessing any sin we find. The Bible tells us, "But if we confess our sins to him, he is faithful and just to forgive us our sins and to cleanse us from all wickedness. If we claim we have not sinned, we are calling God a liar and showing that his word has no place in our hearts" (1 John 1:9-10).

3. *We must remember the standards God has set.* The Ten Commandments were placed under the atonement cover, the mercy seat, because they are the heart of God's standards. God expects us to search His Word constantly so that we can learn and remember His commands to us.

4. *We are to plead for others around us.* The main job of the high priest was to offer sacrifices on behalf of the sins of the people. Similarly, our prayer life should be one of intercessory communication with God for others. We should pray for the salvation of unbelievers. And we should pray about the spiritual growth, trials, and temptations of our brothers and sisters in Christ.

Living a Life that Matters

Our holiness inevitably leads to reactions from those around us. In his book *The Holiness of God*, R.C. Sproul observes that some unbelievers feel uneasy in the presence of an obedient Christian. The holiness of God reflected in a believer's life makes the non-Christian uncomfortable. Sproul tells the following story to illustrate his point.[7]

A well-known professional golfer was playing in a tournament with President Gerald Ford, Jack Nicklaus, and Billy Graham. After the game one of the other men on the tour asked the golfer what it had been like to play with President Ford and Billy Graham. The pro said after a string of curses, "I don't need Billy Graham stuffing religion down my throat."

Had Billy Graham badgered the man? Had Graham tried to coerce him?

Sproul commented, "Astonishing. Billy Graham had said not a word about God, Jesus, or religion, yet the pro stormed away after the game accusing Billy of trying to ram religion down his throat."

What had happened? Simply this: The evangelist had so reflected Christ's likeness that Graham's presence made the pro feel uncomfortable. If we are identified with Christ and walk in holiness, unbelievers will sense our godly influence—before we even mention religion.

On the other hand, some unbelievers will respond positively to our godly influence, asking us about our faith. In many witnessing situations, people find that others are eager to begin a relationship with God but they just don't know how. When they see Christ's love displayed, they are willing to open themselves up to the message of salvation.

A Life-Transforming Truth

I truly believe that one reason more people are not excited about living a holy life is because they do not see how following Christ closely leads to excitement and joy. C.S. Lewis once commented to an American friend, "How little people know who think that holiness is dull. When one meets the real thing...it is irresistible. If even 10 percent of the world's population had it, would not the whole world be converted and happy before a year's end?"[8] Holiness is not a matter of human rules that hang around our necks like so many chains. Holiness is walking in the intimate, radiant light of the Son of God, where there is overflowing blessing, peace, and fulfillment.

Many people, however, struggle with living holy lives. Do not worry if that is the case for you. We all struggle at different times in our Christian walk. No one is perfect. This is why it is important to understand that sanctification is a process—something we will be working on until the Lord takes us to heaven. The apostle Paul writes, "And I am certain that God, who began the good work within you, will continue his work until it is finally finished on the day when Christ Jesus returns" (Philippians 1:6).

The process of sanctification can be compared to an iceberg, which is almost 90 percent under water. As the sun shines on the iceberg, the exposed part melts, moving the lower part upward. In the same way, we are usually aware of only a small part of our sinfulness and need, which is all we can deal with at any one time. However, as the light of God's work in our lives changes us in the areas we know about, we become aware of new areas needing the work of God.

In the process of sanctification, God's Word assists us in our spiritual battle. As we study His Word, God by His Spirit is conforming us in attitude and in behavior to the person of Jesus Christ. The result is that God is restoring in believers the spiritual qualities of the image of God, qualities that were marred when Adam and Eve sinned.

How God works out the process of sanctification in your life is a unique relationship between you and God. For Jim, it meant dealing with his attitudes about shirking duties at work. He was a fireman, but as soon as he received his permanent placement, he found many ways to avoid being put on certain cleaning and cooking details. He knew his attitude caused resentment with other members of the crew, but he was good at ignoring the looks and comments he got. But then the Lord began to stir up Jim's conscience about his laziness. While reading the book of Proverbs one day, Jim came across several warnings against laziness. He was convicted about his sin and committed himself to changing his habits, confessing his old attitude and asking God to give him a new one.

It was hard at first. The desire to get out of doing those menial chores had a hold on his heart. But slowly, through much prayer, Jim began dealing with his problem. Eventually, he felt such joy and peace about his relationships at work. As he took his focus off his own self-centeredness, he began to become more concerned about the needs of others.

Friend, you are God's holy temple, His dwelling place. With this glorious privilege in mind, begin living for Him in all you do.

DISCOVER THE TREASURE

Since our chapter was about holiness and how the Tabernacle pictures God's holiness, we will study the life of the first high priest, Aaron, who was the brother of Moses. Again, use the 4Ts map for your study.

Since the story of Aaron spans several books of the Bible, let's look at a few passages to understand who Aaron was. If you consult a concordance for the verses that mention Aaron, you would find more than three hundred verses. Instead of reading all those verses, concentrate on what you learn about Aaron from the following passages. Then answer the 4Ts questions, which have been adapted for this biographical study.

Read:

Exodus 4 to discover how Aaron came to be a leader.

Exodus 17:8-16 to discover Aaron's role in a key battle.

Exodus 28 to discover Aaron's role as a high priest.

Numbers 12 to discover Aaron's sin and its consequences.

Numbers 16 to discover Aaron's spiritual role on behalf of disobedient people.

Then:

Perspective: What historical and cultural setting and background did Aaron live in? How did this influence his life? (Discover this first from the passages themselves, but you may also want to check a Bible dictionary, study notes in a study Bible, or other resources to understand historical details about the setting and background.)

People: What do we know about Aaron? What did he accomplish during his lifetime? Did he experience a great crisis? How did he face it? What are his outstanding personality traits? What were his strengths and weaknesses? Who influenced him? Whom did he influence? (Again, discover what you can from the passages themselves. *After* you are finished with your personal study, you may want to consult a Bible dictionary or study notes, but don't let those do your thinking for you.)

Timeless:

Preview: What is similar between the problems Aaron faced and the problems we face today?

Principles: What are the lessons to be learned? What biblical principles did Aaron use to grow to spiritual maturity?

Today:

Purpose for today: How do the timeless truths and lessons apply to today's society?

Pattern: How are the people and situations the same today as they were in Bible times?

To me:

Promises: What possible promises can I claim from the study of Aaron's life?

Practical application: What example does Aaron set for me? Does his life story convict me of a sin I need to confess?

Prayer: Is there a prayer for me to echo?

Prayer Points:

16

How Does the Bible Help My Love Grow?

What do we think of when we hear the word *love*? We hear the word used frequently in everyday conversation:

"I love your dress."

"I love lasagna."

"I love your suggestion."

"I love vacationing in Hawaii."

"I love van Gogh paintings."

"I love my professor."

"I love my roommate."

"I love the guy in my office."

"I love my care group."

"I love my spouse."

What are we saying when we make these statements? Most often we are referring to

- A like or dislike—the feeling we get when we desire food, a state of mind, or a material possession, such as "I love chocolate!"

- Friendship—the feeling we get from someone who affirms us or does something else to make us feel good

- Romantic love—the feeling we get in the pit of the stomach when we think of being close to someone

What does the Bible say about love? What is a biblical worldview of love? How does God see love? How do the expressions listed above compare to God's love? They aren't even in the same category.

In chapter 11, we studied what the Bible says about God's love. It is unconditional, with no strings attached, and it involves action. "For this is how God loved the world: He *gave* his one and only Son, so that everyone who believes in him will not perish but have eternal life" (John 3:16, emphasis added). "God *showed* how much he loved us by *sending* his one and only Son into the world so that we might have eternal life through him" (1 John 4:9, emphasis added). This is how Isaiah describes the suffering love of Jesus Christ:

> He was oppressed and treated harshly,
>   yet he never said a word.
> He was led like a lamb to the slaughter.
>   And as a sheep is silent before the shearers,
>   he did not open his mouth...
> But it was the LORD's good plan to crush him
>   and cause him grief.
> Yet when his life is made an offering for sin,
>   he will have many descendants.
> He will enjoy a long life,
>   and the LORD's good plan will prosper in his hands.
>   (Isaiah 53:7,10)

The Bible's standard for love follows this pattern:

1. It is based on an unconditional commitment to another person.

2. It is shown through acts of love and sacrifice.

3. It reaps great joy and peace in the hearts of those who love.

This is the pattern God expects us to use in our relationships with all other human beings. Because God set the example, we have a model to follow. God's Word shows us that model through the sacrificial life of Jesus Christ and through the actions of many other people. If we study

God's pattern outlined in the Scriptures, our ability to love will grow and our lives will change.

Loving God

Our first priority is to love God. Jesus said, "'You must love the LORD your God with all your heart, all your soul, and all your mind.' This is the first and greatest commandment" (Matthew 22:37-38). Loving God means totally surrendering every part of your life to Him.

Do you love the Lord with everything you have and are? How does your love for God express itself in your day-to-day life? Are you so committed to God that you think of Him first when you are making decisions? Do you show Him your love through acts of love and service? Do others around you benefit from your love for God?

My dear friend Lloyd Ogilvie, who was chaplain of the US Senate, tells a story of how he discovered the truth of loving God wholeheartedly. One day, he went on a solitary retreat on a beach. As he was studying the book of John, God challenged him about his aggressive, self-assertive addiction to human power. He relates:

> During those days, the secret of true power became real to me. The pre-existent, reigning, all-powerful Christ is also the indwelling Lord. The glory promised was a manifestation of Christ in me, a character transplant so that I could be like Him in attitude, action, and reaction. A liberating conviction captured my mind: *Christianity is not only life as Christ lived it; it is more than my life in Him; it is Christ living in me.*
>
> I had read those Scriptures before. How had I missed the experience of these promises? The Lord wanted a surrender of all there was of me—mind, soul, will, and body—to Him. It took the crisis of powerlessness to make me ready to receive what was offered all along.
>
> I got on my knees and asked Christ to indwell my total life. I prayed, "Lord, I've missed the secret. I've been ministering *for* You and have not allowed *You* to work *through*

me. Come live Your life in me. I am empty and need to be filled. Love through me; care through me; preach through me; lead through me. All that I am or ever hope to be, I yield to you."

Christ's presence flooded my entire being, from the top of my head to the soles of my feet. I felt loved, forgiven, empowered...

I returned home a different person, set free from my compulsive efforts to try to earn my status with the Lord. The experience replenished the parched places of my soul that had kept my Christian life a constant dry spell. The indwelling Christ gave me all that I had previously worked so hard to achieve, studied to understand, and struggled to accomplish. Now I was free to love without restraint and felt a new boldness, an exuberant joyousness beyond my understanding.[9]

Over the years after that experience, Lloyd reaffirmed this commitment to God many times. He has seen God loving in and through him in so many ways. The change was one of priority—putting God first in everything.

Love Your Neighbor

The second part of the Great Commandment Jesus gave us in Matthew 22 goes like this: "A second is equally important: 'Love your neighbor as yourself.' The entire law and all the demands of the prophets are based on these two commandments" (Matthew 22:39-40). That's the importance God places on our responsibility to love people—all kinds of people, no matter how difficult they are to love.

I have worked with Ney Bailey for forty years. She is a dynamic speaker who helped to begin two of the ministries under the Campus Crusade for Christ umbrella. She tells the story of how much her father had hurt her when she was young and how their relationship deteriorated over the years. She resented him deeply.

One day while studying the book of Romans, Ney was struck with the Bible's definition of faith. She realized that faith is taking God at His Word, so she committed herself to doing what God said.

Then she began to think about her father and how the type of love she had for him did not come close to the love described in 1 Corinthians 13:4-8:

> Love is patient and kind. Love is not jealous or boastful or proud or rude. It does not demand its own way. It is not irritable, and it keeps no record of being wronged. It does not rejoice about injustice but rejoices whenever the truth wins out. Love never gives up, never loses faith, is always hopeful, and endures through every circumstance. Prophecy and speaking in unknown languages and special knowledge will become useless. But love will last forever!

Ney was frequently irritated with her dad and often lost patience with him. Because of some things he had done in the past, her love for him had not been hopeful.

Ney realized that God loves her father unconditionally in spite of all his failings, so she must too. Although the hurtful things her father had done were wrong, her unloving response was also wrong. As the Lord worked on Ney's heart, she decided to ask her father's forgiveness.

> On the weekend I went home, I knew enough not to talk to him during the football game, so I waited for halftime and for my mother to leave the room. When he and I were alone I said, "Daddy, I've been thinking about my growing-up years—how unloving, ungrateful, and unkind I was. Will you forgive me?"

> As he turned and looked at me with a twinkle in his eye, he said, "No." Pausing, he added, "I don't remember all those things except for the time..." And then he named one.

> Knowing the importance of his response, I asked, "Will you forgive me for what you can remember?"

> "Yes," he answered.

From that time on, he was warmer and kinder than ever before.

Without warning, a few years later my father became critically ill.

As I was leaving his bedside in the intensive care unit, I said, "Well, Daddy, I'd better go now and let Brenda [my sister] come in. She's out in the hall waiting. I love you, Daddy."

"I love you too, honey, whether you are here or whether you are waiting in the hall to come in." Those were to be his last words to me.[10]

Lloyd and Ney are "heroes of love" in my book. You undoubtedly have your own list of those heroes, people who reflect Christ by the way they love God and others.

Let me list some specific ways that God asks us to carry out our love for Him and for others.

- Loving God means keeping His commandments (John 14:15,23).
- Loving God means loving His Word (Psalm 119:16).
- Loving God means loving our Christian family (John 13:35).
- Loving your neighbor includes loving your enemies (Matthew 5:44).
- Loving your neighbor means sacrificing for him or her (John 15:13).
- Loving your neighbor means treating people equally (Deuteronomy 10:19).
- Loving your neighbor means forgiving him or her (2 Corinthians 2:5-7).

I could list many more. As you study God's Word, you will indeed find many more ways of showing love to others through Christ's example and the commands of Scripture.

Loving by Faith

You may be saying to yourself, *I can think of lots of people I just can't love. How can I change this?* Let me explain how you can joyfully love the most difficult people.

Everything in the Christian life is based on faith. God's Word says, "It is impossible to please God without faith" (Hebrews 11:6). "This Good News tells us how God makes us right in his sight. This is accomplished from start to finish by faith. As the Scriptures say, 'It is through faith that a righteous person has life'" (Romans 1:17). We love by faith just as we received Christ by faith, just as we are filled with the Holy Spirit by faith, and just as we walk in the Spirit by faith. Likewise, there can be no demonstration of God's love apart from faith.

It is God's will for us to love. He would not command us to do anything that He will not enable us to do if only we trust and obey Him. God promises, "And we are confident that he hears us whenever we ask for anything that pleases him. And since we know he hears us when we make our requests, we also know that he will give us what we ask for" (1 John 5:14-15). Relating this promise to God's command to love, I discovered: We can claim by faith the privilege of loving with His love. To experience and share this love, we must claim it by faith; that is, we must trust His promise that He will give us all that we need to do His will on the basis of His *command* and *promise.*

Love is an act of our will and not of our emotions. We must commit ourselves to loving those difficult people, and the feelings of love will follow. Because we are obeying a command of God, we are not being hypocritical when we say "I love you" to a person even though we don't have loving emotions toward that person at the time. When we begin to practice loving others by faith, we will find that problems of tension with other people will disappear, often miraculously.

I encourage you to make a list of the people you find it difficult to love. Then begin to love them by faith. Perhaps your boss, a coworker, your spouse, your children, or your father or mother will be on your list. Confess to the Lord any wrong attitudes you have about those people and your relationship to them. Ask the Holy Spirit to fill you with Christ's love for each of them. By faith draw on God's limitless, inexhaustible, overwhelming love for them. By faith love every one of your "enemies"—those who anger you, ignore you, bore you, or frustrate you. Then, as God enables you, claiming the power of the Holy Spirit, go to the people with whom you have discord and conflict. Tell them that you love them.

You will discover, as I have, that we can never run out of opportunities to love by faith. People are desperately waiting to be loved with God's love. And God has an unending supply of His divine, supernatural love for everyone. It is for us to claim, to grow on, to spread to others, and thus to reach everyone around us with the love that counts—the love that will bring them to Christ Jesus.

As we have learned in this part of the book, the Bible will change your life in building an active faith, tapping into God's power source, living a life of holiness, and loving by faith. As you study and read, meditate and memorize the words of Scripture, you will find yourself being challenged and changed to be more like Christ.

DISCOVER THE TREASURE

For our last study, we will once again use a biographical Bible study method with the 4Ts map. Since this chapter is about love, we will study one of the greatest love stories of all time—that of Ruth and Boaz. Do your study on Ruth. Most of what the Bible tells us about her is in the book named after her. However, also notice that she is mentioned in Matthew 1, and understanding why she is mentioned there is important to your understanding of who Ruth was. Again, we have customized the 4Ts questions to fit this study.

> Read Ruth 1–4 and Matthew 1.

Then:

Perspective: What is the historical and cultural setting and background of the book? What is the emotional/spiritual atmosphere of the story? (Discover this first from the passages themselves, but you may also want to check a Bible dictionary, study notes in a study Bible, or other resources to understand historical details about the setting and background.)

People: How is Ruth related to the other characters in the story? How did the social/political/emotional setting of the story affect Ruth's life? Observe the characters' ages, roles, positions, status in society—anything that will help you understand who the people are. What crisis did Ruth face and how did she handle it? What role did faith play in Ruth's story? What were her strengths and weaknesses? Who influenced her? Whom did she influence? (Again, discover what you can from the passages themselves. *After* you are finished with your personal study, you may want to consult a Bible dictionary or study notes, but don't let those do your thinking for you.)

Timeless:

Preview: What is similar between the problems Ruth faced and the problems we face today?

Principles: What are the most important lessons to be learned? What do they teach about the Father, Son, and Holy Spirit? What biblical principles did Ruth use to grow to spiritual maturity?

Today:

Purpose for today: How do the timeless truths apply to today's society?

Pattern: What solutions that Ruth applied still work today? What steps to joy and victory are still effective today?

To me:

Promises: What possible promises can I claim from this passage?

Practical application: What example does Ruth set for me? Does the passage convict me of a sin I need to confess?

Prayer: Is there a prayer for me to echo?

Prayer Points:

17

The Challenge

As we come to the final chapter, we can sum up all we've learned with one question: Are you living by the book, by the Word of God?

I'm sure that you will agree that we live by certain principles and rules in every part of our lives—or we face the consequences. If we drive west down an eastbound freeway, we take our lives in our hands. The traffic rules are imposed for an essential reason: to save lives. Again, if we tried skydiving without a parachute, we would face inevitable consequences. That would be our last sky dive.

The principles and rules instituted in God's Word are there for our benefit. They are an expression of God's love for us. These rules serve as a protecting hedge around our lives. Consider the baby boy born with birth defects resulting from a sexually transmitted disease. His entire life is affected by the moral rules his parents broke. What about the woman who overdoses on illegal drugs? Her life is threatened because she disregarded the chemical and biological rules that sustain life. How about the teenager who kills someone and lives not only with the prison sentence but also with the burden of guilt?

Some ways we break God's rules have consequences that may seem more subtle, yet they reap grave rewards. Look back into your life. What godly principles have you ignored? What consequences have you had to face as a result?

But let's also look at the other side of the spiritual coin. What benefits do we gain by doing things God's way? When we obey God's rules about keeping sexual activity within the boundaries of marriage, we not only greatly reduce the risk of sexually transmitted diseases but also enjoy the pleasures of sexual experience in the context of a safe and committed relationship. When we respect the biological order to our lives and appropriately use only prescribed medicines, we benefit from their therapeutic effect. When we respect the sanctity of life, we live in harmony with other people, free of guilt.

These scenarios bring out the contrast between ignoring God's Word and embracing it. The Bible is God's love letter to us, but we must read it, study it, and apply it to our daily lives so that it can fill us with joy. When we do, we not only avoid many pitfalls but also live an adventure with God that is beyond imagining.

Living by God's Word is not a new concept. When we build our lives on God's Word, we follow the wisdom of those who lived before us. On June 6, 1867, President Ulysses S. Grant wrote from Washington to the editor of the *Sunday School Times* in Philadelphia: "My advice to Sunday schools, no matter what their denomination, is: Hold fast to the Bible as the sheet anchor of your liberties; write its precepts in your hearts, and practice them in your lives. To the influence of this Book are we indebted for all the progress made in true civilization, and to this must we look as our guide in the future."[11]

Today we can find the same commitment to God's Word in the writings of contemporary Christian leaders. Rick Warren, author of the best-seller *The Purpose-Driven Life,* wrote about the importance of living by the Bible: "Fortunately, there is an alternative to speculation about the meaning and purpose of life. It's *revelation.* We can turn to what God has revealed about life in his Word. The easiest way to discover the purpose of an invention is to ask the creator of it. The same is true for discovering your life's purposes: Ask God."[12]

By now you have uncovered some life-changing truths during the Bible studies you completed as you've read this book. This is just a beginning—your launchpad for truly abundant living.

I want to leave you with two final points that can sum up your ongoing interaction with God's Word:

1. Keep your commitment to God's Word strong.

2. Share your commitment with others.

It's that simple. You now have the tools—ways to read and study the Bible—that will give you a lifetime of enjoyment and spiritual growth. It's up to you now to practice the skills you have developed.

Keep Your Commitment Strong

Someone with deep convictions—for good or for bad—can change the world. We've seen examples from history. George Washington helped launch the greatest democracy in history through his commitment to the ideals laid out in the Declaration of Independence and the American Constitution. On the other hand, Karl Marx planted the seeds for Communism, which gave rise to totalitarian tyranny in many parts of the world. His influence led to the deaths of millions in Russia, Cambodia, Vietnam, and China. William Carey helped jump-start a worldwide missionary movement leading to the spread of the gospel among formerly unreached people of India. Charles Darwin influenced generations of our brightest scientific minds to reject God and embrace atheistic evolution.

Do you remember the story *Mutiny on the Bounty* by Charles Nordhoff and James Hall? Unhappy with Captain Bligh, the crew of the British ship *Bounty* staged a mutiny and set the captain adrift in the South Seas. A sequel to that story is *Pitcairn's Island*, the tale of nine *Bounty* crewmen who, along with several Tahitian men and women, sailed to the uninhabited island of Pitcairn and set up a colony.[13] In a short while, the colony devolved into unimaginable debauchery. In a near constant state of drunkenness, the men ended up killing each other until only two former crewmen remained: Alexander Smith and Edward Young.

One day Smith found a Bible among the possessions of a dead sailor. He was curious about the book, but because he was illiterate, he had to rely on Young to read the book to him. Young eventually taught Smith to read the Bible, and soon after that Young died, leaving Smith alone with the island's women and children.

Smith became absorbed in the Bible's message, and it changed his life. He was so committed to the Scriptures that he taught the women and children about God's character and His will for their lives. Smith instituted daily prayer and Sunday worship as a part of the colony's spiritual life.

Twenty years later an American ship landed on Pitcairn Island and found a small colony of godly people living in decency, prosperity, harmony, and peace. How was it accomplished? Through one man's strong commitment to the study of the Bible.

Our commitment to God's Word will unleash powerful forces that not only will change lives but also will shape society.

Share Your Commitment

In the barren Mojave Desert between Los Angeles and Las Vegas stands a three-hundred-foot tower that holds a black receiver forty-five feet high and twenty-three feet across. During the daylight hours, a brilliant ball of fire glows from the top of the tower, creating what was at one time the world's largest solar-powered electrical generating station, Solar One.

How can a black receiver turn into a glowing ball with a temperature exceeding 1,175 degrees Fahrenheit? The secret is on the ground. The desert floor surrounding the tower holds 1,818 computer-controlled frames. Each frame holds twelve giant mirrors that track the sun from the time it rises until it sets.

When sunlight strikes these mirrors, called heliostats, they reflect the sunlight onto the black receiver at the top of the tower. The heat generated at the receiver is transformed into electrical energy through a system of thermal storage and a turbine generator. The tremendous power generated by the station is possible only because the heliostats reflect the sun.

We as Christians—the body of Christ—generate even more power because we reflect the Son, the Lord Jesus. And when we do, God's love and power light up a world that is dark with sin and despair.

We live in a world of rapid and radical change. People's hearts are filled with fear and dread, frustration and hopelessness. We have proven that we are capable of making unprecedented technical advances, but we are often incapable of managing our own hearts or coping with the pressing problems of our time.

What an hour for Christians to reflect the love of Christ! We can become involved in the greatest spiritual harvest since New Testament times. This dark hour in the history of mankind is also an hour of destiny, a time of unprecedented opportunity for Christians to shine as lights in the darkness. This is the hour for which we were born—to set in motion a mighty, sweeping spiritual revolution that will turn the tide of sin and despair and reveal to the world that the glorious gospel of our Lord Jesus Christ offers the power to change the way we live.

Since the inception of Campus Crusade for Christ, its purpose has been to help fulfill the Great Commission. Obedience to this all-important mandate is indeed the primary means that God has given His church to change the world and its cultures. When we faithfully take the gospel to the nations, the transformed lives of men and women become vehicles through which Christ dramatically alters the cultural landscape.

I can think of no better way for people to live than to make the Bible and the Great Commission the organizing principles for everything they do in life. When your priority is to obey God's call to live as salt and light in the world, you can have confidence that you are living a biblical worldview and giving glory to God. You can know that you are a transforming influence in every area of culture and society. Offering yourself as a vessel that God can use to lead others to Christ is the greatest thing you can do to help change the world.

The only way to bring real and lasting change to our corner of the world and to our culture is through the church's obedience to the Great Commission and the Word of God. For the culture to change, people must discover the new life that God has for them, or else all our efforts at cultural renewal will result in little more than placing a bandage on a festering wound.

Will you make the Bible and its Great Commission the controlling and guiding principles of your life today? It will be the commitment that transforms your life.

DISCOVER THE TREASURE

If you have done the Bible studies suggested in this book, you have discovered several Bible-study methods that will help you throughout your life: chapter study, book study, topical study, and biographical study. You have practiced using two different "maps" in your study: the "say, mean, apply, fit" map and the 4Ts map.

Everyone needs a balanced diet for good spiritual nourishment. You will probably want to vary your methods between the many methods and maps. But above all, persevere. Stay at your Bible study even when it becomes difficult. In a road trip, some stretches of highway will be difficult to travel. You may have to climb mountains or navigate through rainstorms. Other times you will get weary. But those times will fade in the joy of discovering something you have never before seen or experienced.

The same is true of your Bible study. Make it a daily discipline. Look to the Bible for your nourishment, for direction, for comfort, for life. When you discover the book God wrote, you will discover the God who wrote it. Knowing God and obeying His Word will be more thrilling than any challenge you have ever undertaken.

APPENDIX

Summaries of the Books of the Bible

These summaries of the books of the Bible will help you not only gain an overview of the Bible's whole message but also see each book in the larger context of the whole message. These summaries are adapted from *The Bare Bones Bible Handbook* by Jim George (Eugene, OR: Harvest House Publishers, 2006), and are used by permission of the author.

THE OLD TESTAMENT

The Historical Books

The first 17 books of the Bible trace the history of man from creation through the inception and destruction of the nation of Israel. In the Pentateuch (the first five books of the Bible), Israel is chosen, redeemed, and prepared to enter a promised homeland. The remaining 12 historical books record the conquest of that land, a transition period in which judges ruled over the nation, the formation of the kingdom, and the division of that kingdom into northern (Israel) and southern (Judah) kingdoms, and finally the destruction and captivity of both kingdoms.

Genesis

The Hebrew word for Genesis means "in the beginning," and that is exactly what Genesis is all about. As the first book of the Bible, Genesis lays out the foundations for everything that is to follow, including the key truths God wants you to know in order to make sense of your life. Throughout the pages of Genesis you experience the awesome power of God in His creation, the righteous judgment of God in the flood sent to punish the sinful disobedience of humanity, and the tender mercy of God in His protection of Noah and his family from the flood. You also witness the wondrous grace of God as He sets in motion His plan to redeem humanity, first through the founding of the nation of Israel, and ultimately through the sending of Jesus Christ. Genesis is filled with key moments that form the very basis of history.

Exodus

The time that passes between the final verse of Genesis and the first verse of the book of Exodus is about 400 years. During those four centuries, the 70 members of Jacob's family (who settled with Joseph in Egypt in order to survive a severe famine) multiply to over two million. New kings who do not know of Joseph and his vital role in making Egypt's survival possible are ruling the land. Out of fear of this growing population of Israelites, these new kings force the children of Israel to become slaves. Exodus is a record of God delivering His people from bondage and leading them to Mount Sinai to receive instructions on how to worship and serve Him as God.

Leviticus

By the time the book of Exodus ends, one year has gone by since God's people left Egypt. During that year, two new developments have taken place in God's dealings with His people. First, God's glory is now residing among the Israelites; and second, a central place of worship—the tabernacle—now exists. As Leviticus opens, the Israelites are still camping at the base of Mount Sinai in the wilderness. However, several elements of worship are still missing, and Leviticus contains the instructions for these. A set of sacrifices and feasts are to be observed. Also a high priest, a formal priesthood, and a group of tabernacle workers must be appointed. Leviticus is filled with God's instructions on how His newly redeemed people are to worship.

Numbers

The book of Numbers is written in the final year of Moses's life and concentrates on events that take place in the second and fortieth years after he led the nation of Israel out of Egypt. Everything recorded in Numbers 1–14 occurs in the year after the exodus, and the Israelites' 38 years of wilderness wanderings are condensed into Numbers 15–19. Chapters 20–36 chronicle the fortieth year after the deliverance of God's people. This journey of 39 years from Mount Sinai to the plain of Moab records the experiences of two generations of the nation of Israel.

Deuteronomy

The book of Deuteronomy takes place in one location over about a month of time. Israel is encamped east of the Jordan River across from the walled city of Jericho. It has been 40 years since the Israelites exited Egypt. Deuteronomy concentrates on events that take place in the final weeks of Moses's life. The major event is the verbal communication of God's divine revelation that Moses had received over the past 39-plus years of wilderness wanderings. His audience is the new generation. They are poised and ready to enter the new land. This new generation needs this instruction in order to prosper in their new land.

Joshua

When Moses passed the baton of leadership on to Joshua (Deuteronomy 34), Israel was at the end of its 40 years of wilderness wanderings. Joshua had been Moses's faithful apprentice for most of that 40 years. Joshua's task is to lead Israel into the land of Canaan, drive out the inhabitants, and divide the land among the 12 tribes.

Judges

Judges is a tragic sequel to the book of Joshua. In Joshua, the people were obedient to God and enjoyed victory in their conquest of the land. In Judges, they are disobedient, idolatrous, and often defeated and oppressed. Like the earlier historical books, Judges presents historical facts, but in a very selective and thematic way. Foremost among its themes is God's power and covenant mercy in graciously delivering the Israelites from the consequences of their failures, which they suffered because of their sinful compromises. The book's name refers to 12 unique leaders God graciously raises up to deliver His people when they are oppressed as a result of their disobedience.

Ruth

The book of Ruth takes place during the spiritually dark days of the Judges. Ruth is the story of a woman (named Ruth) who lives during this evil period in Israel's history but does not succumb to its moral decay. Ruth's story is one of integrity, righteousness, and faithfulness. Her story covers about 11 or 12 years. She and Esther are the only women who have books of the Bible named after them.

1 Samuel

We now arrive at a transition in the history of God's people with three sets of "doubles"—1 and 2 Samuel, 1 and 2 Kings, and 1 and 2 Chronicles. These form their own history book, which we could title *The Rise and Fall of the Israelite Monarchy*. Originally 1 and 2 Samuel were one book, but later translations separated them into our present two books. First Samuel is named for the first of three prominent personalities—Samuel, Saul, and David—interwoven throughout its contents.

2 Samuel

Second Samuel picks up where 1 Samuel leaves off. Saul is now gone, so the people of Judah, David's ancestral tribe, declare David as their king, while the northern tribes acknowledge Saul's youngest son as their king. All Israel eventually acknowledges David as their king, and he then reigns in Jerusalem for 33 years. Second Samuel reviews the key events in David's reign with chapter 11 marking the turning point in the life and success of David.

1 Kings

The story of 1 and 2 Kings is basically one of failure. The tiny nation of Israel had gained dominance in its region because God had blessed it. But at the height of their affluence and influence, the people plunged into poverty and paralysis as they turned away from God.

2 Kings

Second Kings continues with the history of the kingdoms of Israel and Judah. They both plunge headlong toward judgment and captivity as the glory of the once-united kingdom fades. When the end finally comes, with the northern tribes taken into Assyrian captivity and the southern tribes deported to Babylon, nine different dynasties are described for the northern kingdom, Israel. But, as promised to David, there is only one dynasty in Judah.

1 Chronicles

First Chronicles covers the same period of Israel's history as the book of 2 Samuel but with one difference. Second Samuel gives a political history of the Davidic dynasty, while 1 Chronicles gives the religious history.

2 Chronicles

The book of 2 Chronicles covers much of the same period as 1 and 2 Kings. It gives a divine editorial on the spiritual nature of the Davidic dynasty from the time of the united kingdom of Solomon to the deportation of the kingdom of Judah, and then to the decree of Cyrus, king of Persia, for the exiles to return to Jerusalem and rebuild the temple. Because this is a spiritual chronicle of David's lineage, the wicked kings of the northern kingdom and their history are omitted.

Ezra

Ezra, the author of 1 and 2 Chronicles, picks up where he leaves off at the end of 2 Chronicles. He records the accounts of two returns of a small remnant of Jews from exile. As a priest, Ezra continues his goal of providing a priestly and spiritual perspective on Judah's historical events. In addition, Ezra believes a record of the building of the second temple could be a helpful reminder of the remnant's link to the first temple.

Nehemiah

Nehemiah provides a sequel to the book of Ezra. First, Ezra arrives on the scene and brings about reforms through the teaching of God's Word. Thirteen years later, Nehemiah, a trusted cupbearer of the king of Persia, arrives in Jerusalem with a burden to rebuild the walls around Jerusalem and to reinstruct the Jewish people, who were becoming pagan through intermarriage with Gentile unbelievers.

Esther

Ezra, Nehemiah, and Esther record God's dealings with the Jews after their prophesied 70 years of captivity in Babylon. While Ezra and Nehemiah deal with the people who returned to Judea, Esther deals with the vast majority who decided to stay in the land of their captivity. Esther is a Jewish girl who by God's sovereignty becomes queen of the Persian Empire that stretched from India to Ethiopia. In the midst of a seemingly hopeless crisis, Queen Esther exerts her influence and the Jewish people are saved from annihilation.

The Poetic Books

Job, Psalms, Proverbs, Ecclesiastes, and the Song of Solomon don't relate historical experiences. Rather they relate the experiences of the human heart. They do not advance the story of the nation of Israel. Instead, through the use of Hebrew poetry, they delve into the questions of suffering, wisdom, life, love, and most importantly, the character and nature of God. And finally, they have another important function—they serve as a hinge linking the history of the past with the prophetic books of the future.

Job

Job probably lived during the same time period as Abraham. Like Abraham, Job is a wealthy and upright man who fears God. Through the fires of affliction—which include the loss of Job's family, his wealth, and his health—a series of debates takes place with his friends over the subject of suffering. Then in a discussion with God, Job is brought to the end of questioning God's actions in his life and trying to justify himself. He finally grasps the majesty, sovereignty, and utter independence of God, and he sees himself as God sees him. He repents of his arrogance, and God restores his health, gives him another family, and makes him wealthier than before.

Psalms

The Psalms are poetic expressions of human and religious feeling, and are divided into five books that comprise a total of 150 individual psalms. The Psalms span the ten centuries from Moses to the days after the Jewish people's exile. They consist of a wide variety of styles and purposes and emotions, such as lament, thanksgiving, praise, worship, pilgrimage, petition, and penitence. Each of the five books ends with a doxology.

Proverbs

While David is the author of a majority of the psalms, his son Solomon is the author of most of the book of Proverbs. Early in his rule, Solomon was granted great wisdom by God. Much of his wisdom is reflected in the 800 proverbs that are included in the book of Proverbs. A proverb is a brief statement that offers a pithy but powerful observation. And it is common for proverbs to use comparisons, contrasts, analogies, or figures of speech to help drive home their point. The object of Proverbs is to inspire profound reverence for God, a fear of His judgments, and a deep love for wisdom and godly living.

Ecclesiastes

This book is an autobiography by King Solomon at the end of his life after he strayed from God. In four "sermons," he describes his search for satisfaction and his discovery that life without God is a long and fruitless search for enjoyment, meaning, and fulfillment. Solomon hopes to spare his readers the bitterness of learning through personal experience that carrying out life's pursuits apart from God is empty, fruitless, and meaningless.

Song of Solomon

In Song of Solomon, a youthful Solomon writes a wedding song to describe his love for and marriage to a beautiful country girl called the Shulamite. This song records the dialogue between an ordinary Jewish maiden and her beloved, the king of Israel.

The Prophetic Books

The next 17 books of the Bible comprise about one-fourth of the Scriptures and make up the last division in the Old Testament. The office of prophet was instituted during the days of Samuel, and those who were prophets stood along with the priests as God's special representatives. The men who wrote these books were called or appointed to speak for God Himself. God communicated His messages to them through a variety of means, including dreams, visions, angels, nature, miracles, and an audible voice. Unfortunately, the messages they shared from God were often rejected and their lives endangered. The prophetic books have four major themes and purposes:

1. To expose the sinful practices of the people
2. To call the people back to the moral, civil, and ceremonial law of God
3. To warn the people of coming judgment
4. To anticipate the coming of Messiah

Isaiah

Isaiah's ministry spanned the reigns of four kings of Judah. He was raised in an aristocratic home and married to a prophetess. He was initially well liked, but, like most of the other prophets, was soon despised because his messages were so harsh and confrontive. In the first 39 chapters, Isaiah stresses the righteousness, holiness, and justice of God, and the last 27 chapters portray the Lord's glory, compassion, and grace.

Jeremiah

Some 80 to 100 years after Isaiah's death, Jeremiah enters the prophetic scene. The book of Jeremiah is an autobiography of Jeremiah's life and ministry during the reigns of the last five kings of Judah. Jeremiah is the last prophet before the fall of Jerusalem. He is called "the weeping prophet" because of his deep sorrow over the unrepentant nation, the upcoming destruction of Jerusalem, and the exile of its people. Jeremiah proclaims not only words of warning but also words of encouragement as he affirms God's promises to renew His people by renewing their hearts.

Lamentations

The book of Lamentations is Jeremiah's eyewitness account of the destruction of Jerusalem by the Babylonian army. Jeremiah predicted this disaster, and now he writes these five funeral poems to express his grief. But Jeremiah also reminds readers that God has not and will not abandon His people. He is faithful, and His mercies continue to remain available to those who respond to His call.

Ezekiel

While Jeremiah is prophesying in Jerusalem that the city would soon fall to the Babylonians, Ezekiel is giving a similar message to the captives already in Babylon. Like the people in Jerusalem, the captives could not believe that God would allow Jerusalem to be destroyed. After the news of the fall comes, Ezekiel changes his message to one of future hope and restoration for the people. Throughout the book, Ezekiel describes his encounters with God's glory.

Daniel

The book of Daniel is written to encourage the exiled Jews by revealing God's sovereign program for Israel during and after the period of Gentile domination. The "times of the Gentiles" (Luke 21:24) begins with the Babylonian captivity. The Jews will suffer under Gentile powers for a long time. But this period is not permanent, and a time will come when God will establish the Messianic kingdom, which will last forever. Daniel repeatedly emphasizes the sovereignty and power of God over human affairs.

Hosea

Hosea is the first of 12 prophetic books called the Minor Prophets—not because they are less important but because of their size. Hosea's ministry begins during a time of prosperity in the northern kingdom. But the prosperity is only external. Inwardly, the people are idolatrous and wicked. In less than 30 years, Israel and its capital, Samaria, would fall. The book details the unhappy union of Hosea and his unfaithful wife, Gomer. Their story serves as a vivid parallel of the loyalty of God and the spiritual adultery of Israel. With empathetic sorrow, Hosea exposes the sins of Israel and contrasts them to God's holiness. The nation must be judged for its sin, but it will be restored in the future because of the love and faithfulness of God.

Joel

Joel lived and ministered in Judah about the same time as Elisha and Jonah ministered in the northern kingdom of Israel. Joel predicts that the land will be invaded by a dreadful army that will make a recent locust invasion seem mild by comparison. On behalf of God, Joel appeals to the people to repent and avert the coming disaster.

Amos

Amos is a shepherd and a cultivator of sycamore trees from a rural area south of Jerusalem. He is divinely commissioned to leave his homeland and preach a harsh message of judgment to the northern kingdom of Israel. He offers eight pronouncements warning of coming disaster because of complacency, idolatry, and the oppression of the poor. But because of the peace and prosperity of Israel during this period, his message falls on deaf ears.

Obadiah

Obadiah, the shortest Old Testament book, is a dramatic example of God's response to anyone who would harm His chosen people. Edom was a mountainous nation to the southeast of Israel. As descendants of Esau, the Edomites are blood relatives of the people of Judah. And, of all people, they should rush to the aid of Judah when it was under attack. Instead, the Edomites gloat over Judah's problems. They capture and deliver survivors to the enemy and even loot Judah's land. Because of Edom's indifference, defiance of God, and treachery, Obadiah gives them God's message of coming disaster.

Jonah

Jonah is the autobiography of a prophet who did not want to preach repentance to Israel's enemy, the godless Assyrians, and their capital city, Nineveh. The book is unusual because it is the only Old Testament book whose message is to a Gentile nation. God declares that His grace is extended to the Gentiles as well as to His covenant people, Israel. Jonah's message is received with almost immediate repentance, and the city of 600,000 people is spared.

Micah

Micah proclaims a message of judgment to a people persistently pursuing evil. He presents his three oracles, or cycles, of doom and hope as if he were in a courtroom. The book begins with judgment for Israel's unfaithfulness and ends on a strong note that the Lord intends to fulfill the unconditional promises He made to Abraham and Jacob.

Nahum

About 100 years after the prophet Jonah had visited Nineveh, the city once again becomes marked by murder, cruelty, idolatry, and social injustice. Nineveh is the capital of the Assyrian Empire, now the most powerful nation in the world and seemingly the most invincible. But no one can stand against God, who is sovereign over all the earth. According to Nahum, because of Nineveh's sins, this proud, powerful nation will be utterly destroyed. The end would come within 50 years.

Habakkuk

Toward the end of the kingdom of Judah, things had gone from bad to worse. This unchecked wickedness causes Habakkuk, a little-known prophet and a contemporary of Jeremiah, to question God's silence and apparent lack of judgment in purging His covenant people. God answers with a torrent of proof and predictions. Habakkuk finally catches a glimpse of the character and nature of God, and can only stand back in awe and praise of Him.

Zephaniah

Zephaniah's preaching ministry may have played a significant role in preparing Judah for the revival that comes with King Josiah, the last good king of Judah. Zephaniah warns of the coming day of judgment, first upon Judah and then upon the Gentile nations. As in the other prophetic books, God also promises to restore the fortunes of His people.

Haggai

Haggai is one of three prophets preaching to the Jewish people who had returned from exile, Zechariah and Malachi being the other two. Prophets of the past had to deal with idolatry, but 70 years of exile had cured the people of this evil. Haggai urges God's people to stop thinking about their own comforts. Instead, they were to put their energies into the restoration of the temple. The people's hearts are stirred, and they take up the work of rebuilding the temple. God then honors their reshaped priorities and blesses their personal lives.

Zechariah

Zechariah's prophetic ministry overlaps that of his older contemporary, Haggai. The first eight chapters of Zechariah are written to encourage the remnant while they were rebuilding the temple. The last six chapters are written sometime after the completion of the temple in anticipation of Israel's coming Messiah. This book is second only to Isaiah in the volume of material about the Messiah, the Lord Jesus Christ.

Malachi

Malachi is probably a contemporary of Ezra and Nehemiah. He attacks the evils that arise in Jerusalem after the temple is rebuilt and its services are reestablished. Malachi's message of judgment on Israel for their continuing sin is the last word from God for 400 years until another prophet arrives with a message from God. God promises that one day in the future, when the Jews repent, the Messiah will be revealed and God's covenant promises will be fulfilled. The 400 years of silence is broken when John the Baptist preaches, "Repent, for the kingdom of heaven is at hand!" This was a declaration that the long-promised Messiah had come!

THE NEW TESTAMENT

The Historical Books

The New Testament is a collection of 27 books that reflect a wide range of themes, literary forms, and purposes. The first five books—Matthew, Mark, Luke, John, and Acts—are entirely narrative and the only historical books in the New Testament. The first four books, or the Gospels, are a historical account of the life of Jesus Christ, the Messiah, whose birth, life, death, and resurrection were prophesied throughout the Old Testament. The book of Acts provides a factual report of the period from Christ's final words to His followers and His ascension into heaven to the travels and trials of the apostle Paul. Acts describes some of the key events in the spread of the "good news" from Judea to the far reaches of the Roman Empire.

Matthew

It has been 400 years since Malachi gave his last words of prophecy. Control of the land of Israel has passed from Medo-Persia to Greece and now to Rome. Greek is still the official trade language of the people, and it is the language in which the New Testament is written. Matthew is a tax collector until Jesus calls him to become one of the 12 apostles. Now, more than 20 years since Jesus's return to heaven, the good news has traveled the length and breadth of the Roman world. The Jewish Christians are starting to be persecuted, and Matthew wants to strengthen their faith and provide them with a tool for evangelizing the Jewish communities throughout the Roman world. He presents Jesus of Nazareth as Israel's promised Messiah and rightful King. With the King comes His kingdom—the kingdom of heaven—which will be occupied by those who acknowledge and obey this King.

Mark

Mark was not an eyewitness of the life of Jesus, but he is a close companion of the apostle Peter, who passed on the details of his association with Jesus to Mark. Whereas Matthew wrote his Gospel to a Jewish audience, Mark seems to target Roman believers. Mark presents Jesus as the Suffering Servant. He focuses more on Jesus's deeds than His teachings. He demonstrates the humanity of Christ and describes His human emotions, His limitations as a human, and ultimately His physical death.

Luke

Luke's Gospel is addressed to a man named Theophilus. Its purpose is to give an accurate historical account of the unique life of Jesus. Luke, a doctor and the only Gentile author of the New Testament books, is writing to strengthen the faith of Gentiles, especially Greek believers. He also desires to stimulate unbelieving Greeks to consider the claims that Jesus Christ is the Perfect Man—the Son of Man—who came in sacrificial service to seek and save sinful men.

John

It has now been 50 years since John witnessed the earthly life of Jesus. The Christian faith has flourished and spread throughout the known world, but with growth has come great persecution by the Roman government. All Christ's apostles have died or been martyred except for John. Now an old man, John provides a supplement to what has already been written about Jesus in the first three Gospel accounts. His account of Jesus presents the most powerful and direct case for the deity and humanity of the incarnate Son of God. Taken together with the other Gospels, a reader will have a complete portrait of Jesus, the God-man. In Jesus, perfect humanity and deity are fused, making Him the only possible sacrifice for the sins of mankind.

Acts

As a sequel to his account of the life of Jesus, Luke continues the history of what happens after Jesus returned to heaven. In Acts, the church starts with just 120 people, but with the coming of the promised Holy Spirit, these few become empowered and boldly witness to all who would listen of the life-changing message of Jesus's resurrection. In spite of severe opposition and persecution, the fearless church experiences explosive growth. Acts 1:8 provides an outline for following Luke's 30-year record of the growth of the church, which begins in Jerusalem, spreads to Samaria, and extends to the world.

The Doctrinal Books

The Bible moves to 22 letters (epistles) that provide teaching and instruction in Christian truth and practice. The first nine epistles (Romans through 2 Thessalonians) are penned by the apostle Paul and contain many of the essential doctrines of the Christian faith. They are all addressed to Christian assemblies or churches. The four that follow (1 Timothy through Philemon) are also written by Paul but are addressed to individuals. Their contents center on personal relationships.

The final nine letters of the New Testament (Hebrews through Revelation) are addressed to groups scattered throughout the world. Their messages address the issues of persecution, false teachers, the superiority of Christ, and His soon return. Even though the book of Revelation focuses largely on God's plan for the future, it is also a letter of Jesus Christ, transmitted through the apostle John, affirming Christ's authority and His concern for the church. Revelation closes with a wonderful glimpse of Christ's righteous reign on the new earth.

Romans

Toward the close of his third missionary journey, Paul writes this letter to the church in Rome from the Greek city of Corinth. He writes not to correct any doctrinal error, but to introduce himself to the church at Rome so the people can pray for him, encourage him, and help him with his future plans to minister in Spain. But being the teacher he is, Paul can't help but also teach his new friends about the righteousness that comes from God—the great truths of the gospel of grace.

1 Corinthians

While the apostle Paul is teaching and preaching in Ephesus (a city in what is now modern Turkey), visitors arrive from the church at Corinth, a church he had planted in Greece some three years before. One group of the visitors reports disturbing news of factions, immorality, and lawsuits within the body of believers. Another group comes with difficult questions concerning marriage and divorce, eating food offered to idols, matters of public worship, and the resurrection of the body. Using his God-given power and authority as an apostle, Paul writes this first of two letters to believers in Corinth to firmly address their deplorable conduct and answer their questions.

2 Corinthians

After writing 1 Corinthians, Paul plans to stay at Ephesus a little while longer before going on to Corinth. His stay, however, is cut short by a riot of the tradesmen over the effect Christianity is having on the sale of idols. Paul sends his young disciples, Titus and Timothy, ahead to find out what effect his exhortations are having on the Corinthian believers. As Paul travels toward Corinth, Titus finds him and reports that the Corinthians have repented of their resistance against Paul and his teaching. With great joy, but filled with concerns regarding new threats and smoldering rebellious attitudes, Paul writes this second letter.

Galatians

Paul hears the distressing news that many of the Galatians who had come to belief in Christ have fallen prey to the heresy that Gentile believers must submit to all the Mosaic law before they can become Christians. Paul writes this letter to defend justification by faith alone and warn the churches in Galatia of the dreadful consequence of abandoning the pure gospel of Christ alone for salvation.

Ephesians

Paul founded the church in Ephesus and spent three years teaching its members. Now, some five or six years later, Paul is a prisoner in Rome, awaiting trial before Caesar. While he waits, Paul writes this letter. Unlike some of his other letters, this one is not written to speak of some heresy or specific problem in the church. Instead, Ephesians is a letter of encouragement. In it Paul describes the nature of the church, which is not an organization but a living organism, the body of Christ. He then challenges his readers to function as the living body of Christ on earth.

Philippians

The Philippian church had always given funds to help finance Paul's needs. Having heard about Paul's imprisonment, they send another contribution, and along with it, a man named Epaphroditus to minister personally to Paul's needs. Unfortunately, Epaphroditus becomes ill, almost to the point of death.

Paul, who realizes his own death could be close, writes this letter to thank the Philippians for their gift and sends Epaphroditus home with the letter, in which Paul describes his circumstance in prison, exhorts the believers in Philippi toward greater unity, and warns them against false teachers.

Colossians

Paul had never visited the church in Colossi, but Epaphras, the founding pastor of the church, has come to Rome to visit Paul and report his concerns about a heretical philosophy that is being taught in Colossi. Paul immediately pens this letter to warn the Colossians against this heresy that is devaluing Christ. He writes to give them a proper understanding of Christ's attributes and accomplishments.

1 Thessalonians

Because of the response from many God-fearing Gentiles in Thessalonica to Paul's message of salvation in Christ, jealous Jews quickly turned the townspeople against Paul. To avoid the mob, Paul had to flee under the cover of darkness. Still concerned for these new believers, Paul sends his companion Timothy to see how they are doing while he travels on to Athens and Corinth. Timothy meets Paul in Corinth, and the book of 1 Thessalonians is the result of Timothy's good report from this new church.

2 Thessalonians

This sequel to Paul's first letter to the Thessalonian believers is written just a few months later while Paul is in Corinth. Word came to Paul from Thessalonica that some had misunderstood his teaching about the second coming of Christ. His statements that Christ could come at any moment had caused some to stop working at their jobs and to begin sitting around waiting for Christ's return. Others are viewing their continuing persecution as signs that this must be the last days. Responding quickly, Paul sends this second epistle to the young church.

1 Timothy

Timothy has been one of Paul's closest disciples since he was first recruited for service some 15 years earlier. Paul has just been released from his first imprisonment in Rome, and revisits several of the cities in which he had ministered, including Ephesus. When Paul leaves Ephesus, he asks Timothy to stay behind as his personal representative. Paul hopes to eventually return to Timothy, but in the meantime, he writes this letter to give Timothy practical advice for his pastoral ministry.

2 Timothy

Paul is in prison and aware that the end is near. But before he dies, Paul wants to pass on the mantle of ministry to Timothy, his trusted assistant. Concerned that Timothy may be in danger of spiritual burnout, Paul writes to encourage him to continue being faithful to his duties, to hold on to sound doctrine, to avoid error, to expect persecution for preaching the gospel, and above all, to put his confidence in the Word of God as he preaches it constantly.

Titus

After his release from his first imprisonment in Rome, Paul returns to Crete for ministry and leaves Titus there, who is a trusted and longtime disciple of Paul's. Paul now writes to Titus to give encouragement and counsel to a young pastor who is facing opposition from ungodly men within the newly formed churches. He gives instruction on how those young-in-the-faith believers are to conduct themselves before a pagan society that is eager to criticize this new religion and its people.

Philemon

A runaway slave from Colossi by the name of Onesimus makes his way to Rome and, in God's providence, becomes a Christian under Paul's ministry. Amazingly his master and owner, Philemon, had also been saved under Paul's ministry several years earlier. Now Paul, a prisoner, wants to do the right thing and send Onesimus, his new friend and fellow believer, back to Philemon. Paul writes this letter beseeching Philemon to forgive his runaway slave and receive him back as a new brother in Christ.

Hebrews

Many Jewish Christians find themselves under intense persecution as they try to live out their newfound faith in Christ while living in Jewish communities where the Old Testament is the focus of religion. The unknown writer of the book of Hebrews believes that many Jewish Christians are in danger of slipping back into Judaism because of this growing opposition. They need to mature and become stable in their faith. By demonstrating the superiority of Christ over all the Old Testament rituals and sacrifices, this author exhorts these early believers to stay true to the gospel of Jesus Christ.

James

The book of James is the earliest of the New Testament epistles and was written by James, a leader of the church in Jerusalem. The people in the Jerusalem church had been scattered to a number of Roman provinces due to persecution, and James writes to exhort and encourage them in their struggles. Genuine faith, he explains, will produce real changes in a person's conduct and character. He presents a series of tests by which a person's faith in Christ can be measured. If real change is absent, then readers are to examine their faith to make sure they are not exhibiting symptoms of dead faith—which is really no faith!

1 Peter

Peter writes this letter to Christians throughout the Roman Empire to show them how to live victoriously in the midst of the coming hostility without losing hope, without becoming resentful, and by trusting the Lord and looking for His second coming. Peter believes that if his readers will live obediently in the midst of a hostile society, they can be evangelistic tools in the hand of God.

2 Peter

About three years after he wrote his first letter, the apostle Peter writes a second one, in which he expresses alarm about the false teachers who have invaded the churches in Asia Minor. They have already caused many problems, and Peter foresees that their false teachings and immoral lifestyles will continue to have a disastrous effect on the churches they have infiltrated. Therefore, Peter writes this letter from his prison cell to warn believers about the dangers of false teachers.

1 John

As the last remaining apostle, John's words are highly authoritative among the churches of Asia Minor. In this letter (as well as in 2 and 3 John) he writes to these churches with a pastor's heart. John wants his readers to know they have assurance of the indwelling God through their abiding relationship with Christ. At the same time, he warns that false teachers have entered the churches, denying that Jesus had actually come in the flesh. They openly reject the incarnation of Christ, and John writes from personal experience to correct this error.

2 John

In this second letter John is concerned with the itinerant ministry false teachers are conducting as they seek to make converts in the different churches that are under John's authority. John is writing to a specific woman who may have unknowingly or unwisely shown hospitality to these false teachers. John fears they may be taking advantage of her kindness, and warns her not to show hospitality to any of these deceivers.

3 John

As with 2 John, this letter deals with Christian hospitality. In John's day, church leaders traveled from town to town helping to establish new churches and strengthen existing ones. These church workers depended on the hospitality of fellow believers. This letter includes three different messages about three men: John commends Gaius for his ministry of hospitality; he condemns the self-serving ministry of Diotrephes; and he congratulates Demetrius for his good testimony.

Jude

Jude has a burning passion for the salvation that comes in Christ, but as he writes, he transitions to a matter that is heavy on his heart. Jude is intensely concerned about the threat of heretical teachers in the church and the response that Christians should have to this threat. Therefore, Jude seeks to motivate his readers to wake up from their complacency and take action against false teachers.

Revelation

Now an elderly man, John has been banished to Patmos, a small island in the Aegean Sea off the coast of Ephesus, for his faithful preaching of the gospel. While there, John receives a series of visions that describe the future history of the world. The visions reveal Jesus Christ as the divine Shepherd who is concerned about the condition of the church, as the righteous Judge who will punish the wicked, and as the triumphant King who will establish His kingdom for all eternity.

Notes

Introduction

1. Even though Dr. Bright died during the final revisions and editing of this book, the publisher decided to retain the verb tenses in the present tense to reflect his thoughts in his initial writing of the book.

2. This comment is quoted on several websites. For example, see Henry H. Haley, "Notable Sayings about the Bible," www.bible-history.com/quotes/henry_h_haley_1.html.

3. If you want to learn more about these two schools of translation, see Philip W. Comfort, *Essential Guide to Bible Versions* (Wheaton, IL: Tyndale, 2000), 99-108.

4. Adapted from Comfort, *Essential Guide to Bible Versions,* 235.

Part 1: Why Should I Believe the Bible?

1. Donald L. Roberts, "John Wycliffe and the Dawn of the Reformation," *Christian History*, vol. 2 (1983): 30.

2. John C. Ryle, *Expository Thoughts on the Gospel of John* (London: Hodder and Stoughton, 1908), notes to the preface.

3. David McCullough, *John Adams* (New York: Simon & Schuster, 2001), 19-20.

4. *Today in the Word,* December 1989, 7.

5. Although the original source of this quotation is not known, you can read it at http://blog.gideons.org/2010/12/the-bible-contains-the-mind-of-god/.

6. Arthur W. Pink, *The Divine Inspiration of the Bible* (Swengel, PA: Bible Truth Depot, 1917), 113-14, quoted in Henry Clarence Thiessen, *Introductory Lectures in Systematic Theology* (Grand Rapids, MI: Eerdmans, 1949), 83.

7. Thiessen, *Lectures in Systematic Theology*, 84.

8. Millar Burrows, *The Dead Sea Scrolls* (New York: Gramercy, 1986), 304.

9. Ibid.

10. Saint Gregory the Great, quoted in Pope Leo XIII, "Continuing Encyclical Letter of Pope Leo XIII on the Study of Holy Scripture," *Providentissimus Deus* (November 18, 1893).

11. Michael Lemonick, "Score One for the Bible," *Time,* March 5, 1990, 59.

12. Charles W. Colson, "Written in Stone: Archaeology and the Bible," *BreakPoint* Commentary, October 27, 1999, radio transcript no. 91027 (Reston, VA: Prison Fellowship Ministries, 1999).

13. Bryant Wood, "Is There Any Confirmation of Biblical Events from Written Sources Outside

the Bible?," *Christian Answers Network* (Gilbert, AZ: Associates for Biblical Research, 2001); see http://christiananswers.net/q-abr/abr-a009.html.

14. Bryant Wood, "In What Ways Have the Discoveries of Archaeology Verified the Reliability of the Bible?," *Christian Answers Network* (Gilbert, AZ: Associates for Biblical Research, 1995); see http://christiananswers.net/q-abr/abr-a008.html.

15. Ibid.

16. Ibid.

17. Ibid.

18. George Barna, *The Frog in the Kettle* (Ventura, CA: Regal, 1990), 118.

19. Bruce Wilkinson and Kenneth Boa, *Talk Thru the Bible* (Nashville: Thomas Nelson, 1983), xii.

20. Ibid.

21. J.I. Packer, foreword to Edmund P. Clowney, *The Unfolding Mystery: Discovering Christ in the Old Testament* (Colorado Springs, CO: NavPress, 1988).

22. These powerful words are taken from a prayer known as "Saint Patrick's Breastplate."

23. Thomas Guthrie, quoted in John MacArthur Jr., *Ephesians* (Chicago: Moody, 1986), 368.

24. Jane McClain, "His Word Will Not Return Empty," *Pray!,* July/August 1999, 26.

Part 2: How Can I Understand the Bible?

1. To read the incredible story of Admiral Richard Evelyn Byrd, see Richard E. Byrd, *Alone* (North Salem, NY: Adventure Library, 1996).

2. Although the original source of this quotation is not known, you can read it at www.1timothy4-13.com/files/chr_vik/sayingsmoody.html.

3. Although the original source of this widely quoted advice from Martin Luther is not known, you can read it at the "Bible, study of" link in the sermon illustration site at www.christianglobe.com/Illustrations.

4. Howard G. Hendricks and William D. Hendricks, *Living by the Book* (Chicago: Moody, 1991), 47.

5. James I. Packer, *Your Father Loves You* (Wheaton, IL: Harold Shaw, 1986).

6. *The NIV Theological Dictionary of New Testament Words*, ed. Verlyn D. Verbrugge (Grand Rapids, MI: Zondervan, 2000), 818-820.

7. Adapted from Jennifer Abegg with Becky Hill, "The Revenger's Tale," *Worldwide Challenge,* July/August 2003, 22-26.

8. Hendricks and Hendricks, *Living by the Book*, 285-89.

9. To read the fascinating story of how one man's love for the Word and his children led to the Bible paraphrase that has touched the lives of millions of people, read Kenneth N. Taylor, *My Life: A Guided Tour* (Wheaton, IL: Tyndale, 1991).

10. David W. Balsiger, Joette Whims, and Melody Hunskor, *The Incredible Power of Prayer* (Wheaton, IL: Tyndale, 1998), 304.

11. W.A. Criswell, *Why I Preach That the Bible Is Literally True* (Nashville, TN: Broadman, 1969), 178.

12. Dennis D. Martin, "Spiritual Pragmatists," *Christian History,* Fall 1999, 38-41.

13. "Did You Know?" *Christian History,* Winter 1990, inside cover.

14. Virginia Lieson, "The Popular Educator," *Christian History,* Winter 1990, 26-29.

15. Timothy Dudley-Smith, "Why Wesley Still Dominates Our Hymnbook," *Christian History,* Summer 1991, 11.

Part 3: What Is the Bible About?

1. Information taken from William R. Newcott, "The Hubble Eye," *National Geographic,* April 1997, 2-17.

2. Information taken from Peter A. Rona, "Atlantic Ocean Geysers," *National Geographic,* October 1992, 104-9.

3. Information taken from the video *Unlocking the Mystery of Life* (La Mirada, CA: Illustra Media, 2002); www.illustramedia.com.

4. Quoted in Paul A. Fisher, "Is Science Moving Toward Belief in God?" *The Wanderer,* November 7, 1985; cited in Charles W. Colson with Ellen Vaughn, *Kingdoms in Conflict* (Grand Rapids, MI: Zondervan, 1987), 66.

5. Charles W. Colson, "Astronauts Who Found God," *BreakPoint* Commentary, radio transcript no. 40818 (Renton, VA: Prison Fellowship Ministries, 1994).

6. Ibid.

7. Michael Kirkland, "Analysis: S.C. Has Its Own 10 Commandments," *Washington Times,* 20 August 2003.

8. "The Lord Is the Holy One," *The Praise and Worship Study Bible* (Wheaton, IL: Tyndale, 1997), 890.

9. Joni Eareckson Tada, "Broken," *Worldwide Challenge,* May/June 2002, 27-28.

10. Ibid., 28.

11. Aaron Belz, "A Leopard among the Bannas," *Christian History,* August 2003, 42-44.

Part 4: How Does the Bible Change My Life?

1. This story, told by Ravi Zacharias, is adapted from Brian R. Coffey, *Quick and Easy Guide: The Bible* (Wheaton, IL: Tyndale, 2002), 79.

2. John Barber, *Earth Restored* (Ross-shire, UK: Christian Focus, 2002), 17.

3. John Calvin, *Commentaries on the Epistles of Paul to the Galatians and Ephesians* (Edinburgh: T. Clark, 1854), 262.

4. Story adapted from Paul Eshleman, *The Touch of JESUS* (Orlando: NewLife Publications, 1995), 242-43.

5. Eshleman, *The Touch of JESUS,* 95-96.

6. M.R. DeHaan, *Broken Things* (Grand Rapids, MI: Zondervan, 1948), 29.

7. This story is adapted from R.C. Sproul, *The Holiness of God* (Wheaton, IL: Tyndale, 1998), 67.

8. C.S. Lewis, *Letters to an American Lady* (Grand Rapids, MI: Eerdmans, 1967), 19

9. Lloyd J. Ogilvie, "The Secret of True Power," *The Greatest Lesson I've Ever Learned: Men's Edition,* ed. Bill Bright (Orlando: NewLife Publications, 2000), 162-67.

10. Ney Bailey, "Is My God Bigger Than My Hurt?" *The Greatest Lesson I've Ever Learned: Women's Edition,* ed. Vonette Bright (Orlando: NewLife Publications, 2000), 13-20.

11. Ulysses S. Grant, as quoted in *America's God and Country: Encyclopedia of Quotations,* comp. William J. Federer (Coppell, TX: Fame, 1994), 264-65.

12. Rick Warren, *The Purpose-Driven Life* (Grand Rapids, MI: Zondervan, 2002), 20.

13. To read the full story of life on the island, see Charles Nordhoff and James Norman Hall, *Pitcairn's Island* (Boston: Back Bay Books, 2003).

About the Author

Dr. Bill Bright, fueled by his passion to present the love and claims of Jesus Christ to "every living person on earth," was the founder and president of Campus Crusade for Christ (now Cru). The world's largest Christian ministry, Cru serves people in 196 countries through a staff of 26,000 full-time employees and more than 225,000 trained volunteers working in some 60 targeted ministries and projects ranging from military ministry to inner-city ministry.

Bill Bright was so motivated by the Great Commission, Christ's command to carry the gospel throughout the world, that in 1956 he wrote a booklet titled *The Four Spiritual Laws,* which has been printed in 200 languages and distributed to more than 2.5 billion people, making it the most widely disseminated religious booklet in history. Other books Bright wrote include *God: Discover His Character*; *A Handbook for Christian Maturity*; *Come Help Change the World*; *The Holy Spirit: The Key to Supernatural Living*; *Witnessing Without Fear*; and *The Journey Home.*

In 1979 Bright commissioned the *JESUS* film, a feature-length documentary on the life of Christ. The film has been viewed by more than 5.7 billion people in 196 countries and has become the most widely viewed and translated film in history.

Dr. Bright died in July 2003 before the final editing of this book. But he prayed that it would leave a legacy of his love for God's Word and its power to change lives. He is survived by his wife, Vonette, their sons and daughters-in-law, as well as four grandchildren.